Coming Home

Coming Home

◆

The Return to True Self

Martia Nelson

NATARAJ
PUBLISHING

COMING HOME: *The Return to True Self*
© 1993 Martia Nelson

Published by Nataraj Publishing
1561 South Novato Blvd.
Novato, CA 94947

Cover art and design by Lightbourne Images
Back cover photo by John Forler
Typography by TBH/Typecast, Inc.

The author of this book does not dispense medical advice nor prescribe the use of any technique as a form of treatment for physical or mental problems without the advice of a physician either directly or indirectly. In the event you use any of the information in this book neither the author nor the publisher can assume any responsibility for your actions. The intent of the author is only to offer information of a general nature to help you in your quest for personal growth.

First printing, April 1993
Second edition
ISBN 1-882591-23-2
Printed in the United States of America
10 9 8 7 6 5 4 3 2

*With love and gratitude
to my mother, Virginia,
and to Mrs. Tate*

Acknowledgments

With warmest heart I thank my friend Satyen for giving me the nudge to begin this book. I am deeply grateful to Mary Wyman, Carole Savoy, Siculi Deerfoot, and Linda Thomas for support and feedback in the beginning stages; your encouragement gave me the confidence I needed to proceed. I add extra thanks to Linda Thomas for generously transcribing hundreds of pages of material and for computer assistance above and beyond the call of friendship. To Sue Brown, Karen Koshgarian, Stella Rhodes, Judy Norton, Brad Clark, Ginny Clark, Stephen Francis Martineau, Tom Swindell, Padi Selwyn, Denise Gardner, and Barbara West—thank you for your gracious and insightful manuscript review.

To my father, Bill, thank you for being there when I needed your support. Bob Cronbach, I treasure the innumerable gifts your presence gave me throughout this project. And thank you, Shakti Gawain and Manuela Adelman, for your friendship and stalwart belief in my work.

Great appreciation goes to my editors, Hal Zina Bennett, Leslie Keenan, and Janet Mills, as well as to Katherine Dieter, Marcus Allen, Jane Hogan, and Jim Burns for the care and attentiveness that went into this book.

I especially thank my clients and students for all you have taught me. I am grateful for your trust and for the honor of being allowed to witness to such depth the challenge, the beauty, and the precious vulnerability of the human journey Home.

Contents

Part III
Self-Love:
Your Source of Life

Part IV
Journey into Form:
The Exploration of Limitation

Part V
Creating Your World:
Abundance and Manifesting

Part VI
Enlivened Emotion:
The Healing Power of Intense Feeling

Part VII
Sexuality:
The Embodiment of Spirit

Part VIII
Living the Split:
Redefining Destiny

Part IX
Awakened Personality:
Loyal Servant to Unlimited Spirit

Part X
Planetary Survival:
Facing Challenge in the World

Part XI
You Are the Earth:
Living the One Body

Attunements and Meditations

To make the material as practical and useable as possible, numerous attunements and guided meditations are sprinkled throughout this book. For quick reference, they are listed below by page number. As you work with these suggestions, let yourself be creative in altering them to fit your needs and your sense of truth.

Preface

I've known Martia Nelson for many years. I've watched her go through the evolutionary process she describes in the first part of this book, and I've seen her develop an extraordinary connection with higher guidance as she writes about in part two. I've had intuitive readings from her over the years, and received amazingly clear and accurate insights and advice.

When she sent me the original version of this manuscript, I stayed up almost all night reading it, feeling very excited. I knew it was one of the best metaphysical books I had ever read, and I felt immediately that I wanted to publish it. Due to various factors, I was not able to follow up on that feeling immediately.

A year later she sent me a revised manuscript. Again, I stayed up half the night reading, and once again I was blown away by the clarity and power of the book. Now the time was right. My husband, James Burns, and I had just started Nataraj Publishing. We were pleased to sign Martia as one of our first new authors.

Coming Home is a clear, practical and inspiring explanation of how we can integrate our human experience with our essential spiritual nature and express the potential that dwells within all of us. As I read it, it actually lifts me into an expanded perspective on my life. I have found it very helpful in my own personal process, and I know many others will as well. Anyone who has resonated with my work is likely to love this book. Frankly, at this stage in my life I read very few books of this nature. This one will be on my bedside table for quite some time. I believe it's destined to become a classic.

—*Shakti Gawain*

Introduction

This book comes straight from my heart. I wrote it knowing there are many people who struggle with a split between personality (the everyday self) and spirit (the greater self) without knowing what is happening to them or even what to call it. This split is a gap in our awareness that keeps us overly identified with the material world and out of touch with our inherent spiritual nature. Because our society doesn't teach us about this split, we often don't recognize the personal crisis it can bring about. For many of us, the distress starts as vague feelings that something is missing from our lives; we feel burned out at our jobs or dissatisfied in our relationships, or maybe we can't even identify what is bothering us.

I think for most of us, the distress of our inner split begins on a very subtle level, then builds over the years to a point of crisis. Health problems may surface. Relationships may crumble. We may feel trapped in our jobs. Even if we don't yet understand what is disrupting our lives, we begin to realize we cannot continue on the path we're following. If we are lucky, we find ourselves at a turning point, aware of a reality beyond what we have accepted as our everyday consciousness. We sense that there is more to life, and we become curious.

At first, we may not know how to talk about this greater reality. We may vacillate between doubting its existence and feeling drawn to it. As we venture further, maybe we read some books or attend a lecture or two. As we do, we hear words like *intuition, higher guidance,* and *unconditional love.* When we start looking for definitions, we get answers that confuse us even more. Yet, in spite of it all, something in these new ideas feels right, encouraging us to go on, however puzzling and crazy it might seem.

In the pages ahead, I share what we can do to go through this new territory, coming out with both clarity and trust about what it means to begin living in a greater way. Ultimately, this book is meant to help us integrate the two realities our culture has kept separate—that of the personality and that of the spirit—so that our lives might become richer and fuller. I show that by embracing the personality, yet also expanding beyond it to the higher guidance of the true self, we return meaning, purpose and passion to our lives.

As you read, emotions may surface that you have not yet fully explored or maybe didn't even know were there. If this happens, take good care of yourself and get the support you need. You might want to talk to close friends or to a pastoral counselor such as a minister or rabbi. You might consider joining a support group or finding a good therapist who can guide you through your feelings. Be sensitive to your own needs. Getting comfort and support from trustworthy sources during times of change is essential. Having a well cared for and healthy personality that feels nurtured and safe enables you to stabilize amidst rapid growth and to open to deeper levels of experience.

To help you put new information to practical use, I have provided meditations and what I call *attunements* throughout the book. The attunements are ways to direct your awareness as you go about your day—ways that you can tune into a deeper reality even as you remain at your everyday level of consciousness. The meditations are intended for times when you can take several minutes and allow yourself a longer period of inner exploration. Feel free to personalize these attunements and meditations, using your own wording, imagery, or personal focus.

With love,
*Martia Nelson**

* Martia is pronounced like Marsha

Part I
My Story

◆

I Begin the Return

1

Opening

In 1984 I heard a voice that changed my life. It was my voice, but it came from a place deep within me that I had never known existed. It told me that I was going to have to change my workaholic lifestyle or I was going to die.

I was 34 years old and had spent the last ten years immersed in a career I loved. I had successfully combined roles as co-owner of a small business, director of a personal growth center, and an instructor of bodywork for students in professional training. My unusual work combination allowed me to express a full range of my personality: my business competitiveness, my creativity, and my desire to communicate with people at a nurturing level.

I loved my work, but I had become addicted to it with an intensity I could not control. I worked evenings and weekends, and when I wasn't working, I was thinking about work. I could no longer relax on vacations, so I stopped taking them. When friends called to suggest getting together, my first reaction was irritation that they wanted to intrude on my work time. I rarely was sick, but I rarely felt well either. I should have noticed that the work I had devoted my life to was now draining the life out of me. But I kept going, until the inner voice spoke and I was able to listen.

It happened in a bodywork session I was receiving from a woman, Aminah Raheem, who had been one of my acupressure teachers. Suffering from stress and exhaustion, I lay, fully clothed, on Aminah's massage table as she gently held a series of acupressure points on my body to help me relax. About half an hour into the session, I felt a discomfort, almost an anxiety, in my belly. Aminah put a reassuring hand on my belly and said, "What is your belly saying to you?"

3

To my surprise, I instantly knew my belly's message. It left no room for misinterpretation: "If you do not stop all the work you are doing and learn a new way to live, you are going to die." It went on to explain, "You are ready for work that takes you to a deeper level, to a deeper way of connecting with people. To find this new work, you must stop what you are doing now. You are so depleted that if you do not stop, you will die within a year in an accident, or in twenty years from cancer."

At this point, I had two distinctly different reactions. On one level, I was shocked. I was sobbing and wailing as my body felt the impact of the message. Facing the reality of death, my body was filled with fear and grief more powerful that anything I'd ever felt before. Yet, at the same time there was a place deep inside me that was completely calm and well, untouched by all the emotion. There was no worry, no fear, no disturbance whatsoever. It was a core of grace and peace beyond all distress I might feel. I realized the message was coming from this inner core and everything it was saying was true. Then the message concluded: "Very few people have the opportunity to witness the beginning of their death. You have a choice to make about whether this is yours."

I didn't know it at the time, but this was my first experience of both personality and true self. By feeling the feelings of personality while accepting the greater message from true self, I had empowered myself to make what was perhaps, up to that point, the most well-informed decision of my life. After letting the inner reverberations of that session stay with me for a couple weeks, I quit all my work.

That decision was a huge leap into the unknown. I had no idea what my new work would be, so I lived in free-fall for over a year. During that time, I often felt insecure and afraid as a result of letting go of so much of my "old" life. In giving up my work, I relinquished an identity I had clung to for a decade. Each month I had no idea how I'd get the money to live. I was without a love relationship to give me continuity or comfort. And while I needed support more than ever, I let old friendships drop, feeling that they no longer "fit." It was as though everything that had been real to me before—or, more accurately, had made me real to myself—had become too vaporous to hold onto anymore.

With my external world in such change, I began looking within—into the thoughts, feelings, and beliefs that had been driving me all my life. The details of this inner landscape were fuzzy at first, but I felt pulled to keep looking. Before long, old pain surfaced as my most distressing childhood experiences presented themselves to me, desperate for release. As I relived memories of physical abuse and emotional isolation, I was flooded with old feelings of fear, shame, and helplessness. For weeks at a time, an unrelenting ache in my chest reminded me that I still felt unlovable and alone. With the help of skilled body/mind therapists, and through lonely hours of my own processing, I slowly came to terms with what was happening. All inner injury that had kept me from having a more fulfilling life was now demanding my attention so it could be healed. This process was painful, frightening, and time-consuming, yet it was perhaps the most significant period of my life.

In the midst of my soul-searching, a friend told me about a woman named Linda who did "intuitive readings," in which she communicated information from her higher guidance to help people in their spiritual growth. In the hope of getting greater perspective on what I was going through, I made an appointment for a reading.

Linda's technique was simple. She closed her eyes, went into a light meditation, and attuned her awareness to higher guidance, inviting love and wisdom to come through. The session was fascinating and quite helpful. Her higher perspective took for granted aspects of my spirit that I had only sensed existed, and I felt recognized at a deep level. Toward the end of the session,

Linda told me that I, too, could receive guidance directly, if I chose to. She suggested sitting for ten minutes three times a day, with the intention of quietly listening.

The suggestion that I could directly receive information from a higher source surprised me. I still held the idea that very few people could do this: those who were gifted and somehow chosen for such special work, and those who were fooling themselves and others. Because I didn't identify with either category, I'd automatically excluded myself from the whole possibility.

Being told that I could have contact with a source of expanded knowledge and unconditional love stirred a longing in me that I had never let myself fully feel. I'd lived much of my life with a buried grief, a sense that I had lost something deep within. It had to do with a vague memory of spiritual family, a family that extended beyond the people I knew and even beyond physical form. This family was my true source, and I longed to reconnect with it. My grief at feeling separated from it transcended emotion; it was a spiritual yearning for Home.

After a few weeks of sitting and listening as Linda had suggested, I was getting nowhere. I felt frustrated and disappointed. Why did she tell me I could do this if I couldn't? I phoned her and complained. She listened patiently, then checked in with her guidance. "You're not ready," she reported back.

I hit the ceiling. "If I'm not ready, why did you get my hopes up? Why did you tell me I could do something I can't do?" I wanted to experience the contact so much.

"It's not that you can't do it. You're just not quite ready because there is something you're blocking," Linda said gently.

I started to say, "I'm not blocking anything!" But before I could get the words out, tears streamed down my face. "Oh, I know, it's that I'm going to have to move," I told Linda. "If I really listen, it's clear my deeper self needs me to move out of the area. I'll leave this house that I've lived in for so long and loved so much. Home is so important to me. It's the hardest thing for me to leave." The barrier was broken.

2

Truth

So often in our daily lives we block things we don't want to hear because of the conflict we'll feel. Yet in turning to higher guidance we ask for the truth. To the degree that we want to expand beyond our previous limitations, we long for it. But to the degree that we still want control over the details of our lives, we resist the truth and fear its touch. The pull toward truth is often equaled by our resistance to it; the ambivalence is our reluctance to choose between empowerment and control.

When the truth touches us, every structure in our lives that was built on nontruth is destined for change. When I let the truth in about needing to move away, I finally allowed truth to touch me. My house was my last holdout, the last tangible symbol of my old self that I still clung to. In finally loosening my grasp on the house, I recognized that the inner power guiding me was beyond my control, and its being beyond my control *was the very reason* it could propel me forward. I knew then that my safety was in my trust of this powerful life force, not in my efforts to control it.

I also realized that following higher guidance never means having to do what it wants us to do. Higher guidance never has an agenda of its own to impose. Its service is to help us open to our inner truth and support us in integrating it into our daily living. Our challenge is to give up our tendency to deny our inner truth; only then are we really free to follow it.

3

Personality and True Self

For the first year my contact with higher guidance was like tender young shoots of new growth. I felt vulnerable and protective, sharing what happened with very few people. I was afraid I wouldn't be believed or that old friends would judge me as unworthy of such a precious experience.

I asked for assistance in every aspect of my life, and the response was consistently helpful. I was given a deeper view of each situation, one that was expanded and revealed a purpose greater than I'd been able to see with my ordinary perception. The most amazing thing was that it kept turning out that nothing about my life was really wrong! This was difficult for me to comprehend because my life seemed so obviously topsy-turvy, and my mind frequently told me I was doomed. Yet higher guidance patiently showed me the divinity, love, and hidden order in every situation, introducing me time and time again to the perspective of my true self. My heart recognized this truth, and I began to learn.

My greatest teacher was the experience of living in split realities: personality and true self. Personality is our daily companion, our conscious self that sees the world through the eyes of limitation and dutifully keeps us informed about what we can and cannot do. True self, on the other hand, patiently stands by, offering the unwavering knowledge that a state of vibrant well-being and unlimited possibility is our true nature, a birthright that can be lived if we choose to do so.

I'd like to mention here that the term "true self" is not meant to imply that any part of who we are is false or unreal. All aspects of our being are real in our human experience and have value. True self simply refers to the aspect of our being that is completely aware of its expanded nature no matter what we may be experiencing in our lives.

As I became more aware of my true self, I sensed when I was drawing from that source and when I was not. I realized that my true self had been with me all my life, quietly guiding me along, yet I had not identified with it. My identity had been with my personality. The feelings, assumptions, beliefs, and expectations of my personality had been the yardstick I had used for measuring my success, safety, sanity, and personal well-being.

Now I was in a bind. My personality told me to tighten control of my life. It was panicked by everything I was doing (and not doing). Yet my true self rejoiced in my growth, showing me that I had changed the direction of my life at every level as an entry into something greater.

At times the outer events of my life seemed to invalidate the information I received through higher guidance and I was challenged to choose which source to believe. So for months I lived with *both* realities and their apparently conflicting information. Magically, everything higher guidance told me ultimately turned out to be true, even against seemingly impossible odds. And in spite of my personality's repeated warnings, I did not go broke, did not die, and did not end up crazy or alone. Instead, something within me shifted to incorporate true self into my identity and I learned a new way to live.

4

My Search

The turning point came through a rite of passage tailor-made for me. Because it was my area of greatest resistance—my personality's last stand—the drama unfolded around leaving my house. After I realized I needed to move, I packed most of my belongings and tried to figure out where I would be going. I sensed that a new home was waiting for me, but I couldn't quite sense where. My inner guidance told me that tracking my new home would strengthen me and teach me a new way of living.

After I'd agonized over my dilemma for a few months, the name of a specific town popped into my mind, out of the blue, during a light meditation. I set off for that area a few days later, and when I arrived, I knew it was home. I easily found the right house; the third one I looked at was definitely mine. I made an offer right away and couldn't wait to move in.

Everything was perfect. My offer was accepted. The bank said there would be no problem with my loan. I put my old house on the market and was confident it would sell quickly. In a few short weeks I would leave the crowded city and settle in the country. Cows would live across the street from me! I was delighted with where my intuition was taking me at last.

Then the trouble started. The bank called and told me they'd made a mistake and couldn't possibly approve my loan. Round and round we went; they wouldn't budge. On top of that, my house wasn't selling, though less attractive houses nearby sold within days.

As the deadline for buying my new house approached, things looked grim. People began to tell me the situation was impossible. Banks told me. The realtor trying to sell my old house told me. Even the realtor representing me in buying the new house told me. Well-meaning friends tried to prepare me for the disappointment they saw coming. That was when I learned to hate the often-heard "spiritual" axiom: "When you're doing what's really right, everything happens easily and effortlessly." (I'm here to say now that this is not always true.)

I was torn inside. For the first time in my life I had clearly heard the intuitive voice of true self, recognized it as real, and followed it by taking major action based on its guidance. I had chosen the expansive reality of true self over the restrictive reality of my personality. I had made the shift.

The planned move to my new home felt so deeply right, more right than anything had ever felt. Yet the outer events clearly contradicted that inner certainty. My confidence was shaken. Was I fooling myself about higher guidance being real? Did this mean that I could never really trust myself again?

At my wit's end, I consulted higher guidance once more. Peace and clarity came instantly: "Of course, that's your new house. You found your home, and you will live there. Do not give up on yourself. What appears to be most real often isn't. Everything will work out."

The third time my realtor called to tell me we should admit defeat and cancel my offer on the new house, I was clear. I said, "My guidance has told me that it's all going to work, and I have confidence in that." Who knows what she thought, but she didn't argue anymore.

Finally we found a way to satisfy the bank's concerns, and my loan got last-minute approval. At eight o'clock on the night before the deadline, someone bought my house. Everything happened smoothly and quickly from then on, and I soon moved into my new home. With that move came my first tangible step into the new territory that had beckoned me for so long. I had crossed over, and, with at least one foot firmly planted on new ground, my journey Home had truly begun.

5

The Overview

Why had my transition been so difficult? I had been going through a move into new consciousness. Because part of my transition had included the experience of living in split realities,

I had manifested the clarity of my true self (through my intuition and higher guidance) as well as the resistance within my personality (through the outer obstacles with the house). To the degree I opened to true self, I found my way. And to the degree I allowed the limitations of my personality's old beliefs and fears to restrict me, my outer way was obstructed.

The dynamics had been very simple, though only hindsight allowed me to see it that way. While lost in the drama I had been blind much of the time, feeling my way from moment to moment. Yet that had been the challenge, the true test. Those moments of choosing greater truth and acting on it had strengthened my alignment with true self and had kept me on my path.

6

Seeing

After I'd made the move to my new house I realized that helping others rediscover their true self was to be my new work. Over the last several years, I've used my process of opening to higher guidance to give readings to hundreds of individuals and to give countless workshops and presentations. In each of these, I received valuable lessons in consciousness along with everyone else. Opening to higher guidance, whether for myself or others, has been my primary source of spiritual education. I have been given experiences I would never have thought possible. I am most grateful for the recurring reminder that we are all more than we appear to be.

I am given this lesson whenever I find myself working with a client whose personality clashes with mine (yes, this happens!). One man got on my nerves in the first two minutes by criticizing things in my office. Also, he wanted a very specific focus to his reading, but wouldn't quite tell me what it was. I felt him block me at every turn. Exasperated, I considered referring him to someone else. Instead, I followed an intuitive feeling to go ahead with the reading. As soon as I opened to higher guidance, everything shifted. My perspective deepened and I no longer saw just a difficult person. This man's suffering was the deep pain of having lost touch with the amazing beauty and love he carried within. With the assistance from higher guidance, it felt natural to address this man with love and honor, relating to him as he truly was rather than as he appeared to be.

I have been shown the deeper truth in people so many times that it profoundly affects my sense of who we all are. I do not yet carry this "true vision" with me consciously on a continuous basis, but I have experienced it often enough that it is creeping into my life. All my work is for the purpose of supporting that process of evolving perception for myself and others.

◆ ◆ ◆

This has been my story. The movement into greater awareness has already begun for all of us, and the story each of us lives is a chronicle for our collective journey. Our stories need to be shared. As we tell our stories, we create a compassionate ritual for releasing the limitations of our past and opening to the empowerment that shapes our future. At the same time, we give inspiration and support to other adventurers who, whether timidly or boldly, dare to make the journey, too.

Part II
Higher Guidance

---◆---

Our Link to Spirit

7
What Is Higher Guidance?

My answer to this question has changed over the years as my experience has grown. At first higher guidance seemed to be separate from me, or at least that was the perspective I took. The thought that I might be receiving information from "just myself" horrified me. I now realize I had that attitude because I still identified myself as my personality, which indeed would have been a limited source from which to draw.

My guidance comes from a spirit consciousness that exists in a state of unlimited knowledge and unconditional love. It is an awareness based in unity, a oneness that we share with all things and all beings. We are often unconscious of this unity because our personalities are so identified with form. Yet, the true self within each of us experiences unity and lives from that knowing. At that level, there is truly no separation between higher guidance and us; we are all truly one.

The more I open to this source, the more the dividing line I thought existed between myself and higher guidance fades. At one point I realized that my true self has been on the "council" of higher guidance all along. Then I began seeing that the true self of everyone to whom I gave readings was also on that council. From there I recognized that the higher consciousness of everyone on our planet was part of higher guidance. Although I often refer to higher guidance as "it" or "them," it would perhaps be more accurate to use an expanded form of "us."

Is this source of guidance made up of anyone else in addition to the collective higher consciousness of people living on earth? I believe so. There seems to be tremendous input from divine realms and expansive states of being. My words seem inadequate past this point, and much of this is still beyond my conscious understanding. Yet I can tell that the medium of communication among all contributing beings seems to be the state of unity, the very state toward which our own conscious awareness is evolving.

Another perspective would be to remove all description suggesting personification or individuation and to simply see higher guidance as a unified source of unlimited intelligence, love, and creativity. You may choose to call it God, the Universe, Source, Spirit, the Beloved, Light, or any other term that opens your heart and reminds you that you are a cherished part of the magnificent scheme of life.

How accessible is this source for the general populace? Because we are never really separate from higher guidance, it is available to each of us in every moment. Assistance in our spiritual growth is never withheld or forced; it is simply offered. Through our true self, we choose how to draw on this guidance and put it to appropriate use in our lives.

I have come to believe that we all draw on higher guidance continuously, just as we draw on the life-giving vitality of air with each breath we take. And just as most of our breaths are taken unconsciously, most of our communication with higher guidance is automatic and unnoticed. In spite of our lack of conscious awareness, the air we breathe is still real to our lungs and the guidance we receive is still real to our intuition. We are never truly alone, and somewhere deep within, we know this.

We can easily become more aware of this source of greater consciousness that we draw from so regularly. There are countless techniques and approaches to choose from, yet any experience of opening to true self will lead us there. True self is the entrance into the greater realms. Through true self we open to unlimited being and allow unlimited experience to enter our lives.

8

Where Does Higher Guidance Come From?

At first I believed that higher guidance was outside myself because I had to view it that way to begin trusting it. Yet over the years, I increasingly noticed an inner aspect of my own being that was an exact match of the "external" higher guidance. Focusing on the external source awakened the internal one—and gave me the ability to recognize it.

This blossoming of my inner higher guidance dissolved the separation I felt from external higher guidance. I now see inner and outer higher guidance as one and the same, a continuum of awareness that is omnipresent. As a result, my identity has been altered to include both an increased self-reliance and a greater sense of interdependence with all life.

With internalized higher guidance, it is possible to see the world with a more refined vision and with an unwavering recognition of perfection. We can surrender to life and follow its flow no matter where it takes us, for both inner and outer realities become trustworthy when divinity is apparent everywhere.

The internalized form of higher guidance is our true self. We need do nothing special to get a true self; each of us already has one. Yet if we have lost touch with true self, we may need to do something special to be conscious of it again. Opening to external higher guidance can be very helpful. However, I stress that the primary purpose of external higher guidance is to help us reconnect with the aspect of ourselves that matches it—and then to help us learn to use our internal source more consciously.

Repeatedly relying on external guidance to replace inner guidance is not beneficial in the long run. It creates an imbalance in our lives, with the external source becoming one more addiction we use to avoid ourselves. Higher guidance of a pure nature will not fall for this; it will not give information that takes us further from ourselves. It will, however, be unconditionally generous with information that leads us to true self-love and natural empowerment.

9

Guidance and Its Form

People report wide variations in their experience of higher guidance. Higher guidance has no form of its own: it is beyond form and does not identify with it. Yet as human beings we live in a world of form. Our personality is so identified with it that everything must have some form before we recognize it as real and are able to talk about it. Language is based on form, as are most thoughts. Because we receive conscious awareness of higher guidance through the filter of our personality, we interpret the experience through our individual and collective needs for form.

This happens very quickly and usually unconsciously. For example, if one person's personality feels more able to open to higher guidance that comes in the form of a wizened old man dressed in white robes with an ancient-sounding name, that is what the experience will be. If another person's unconscious need is for a feminine spirit from another planet, that is the form in which guidance will seem to appear. To believe that the guidance is real, still others may need to relate to a being with a strong personality, a sense of humor, and the ability to give factual data about events on earth. Yet, someone who is less attached to personal form may simply experience higher guidance as radiant energy or as creative inspiration. The list of possible variations is limitless.

None of these forms is any better or worse than any other; the form we give guidance doesn't necessarily matter. In fact, as we grow in consciousness, the form in which we experience guidance will very likely change to reflect our new perspectives.

Being so attached to form can sometimes seem limiting, but it is simply a reality of human life at this time. As human beings, we honor our need for spiritual growth by opening to higher guidance, and we honor our personality by doing it through form. Receiving unlimited guidance through form exposes our personality directly to a more refined frequency of consciousness. Through its own language, the energetics of form, our personality is essentially taught to expand its range of perceived reality and permit greater awareness to come into our daily lives.

It is, then, both wise and compassionate that we don't push aside our personality's needs as we open spiritually. Honoring our need for form as we connect with higher consciousness invites our personality to participate in a way that allows it to be touched and transformed by our greatest experiences.

Higher guidance is unconditionally loving and generous, willing to come to us in any way we allow it. It will never force its way through our personality's limitations, nor will it ever pass us up because we are not "evolved" enough to be worthy. Higher guidance honors us *as we are* and graciously works in harmony with both our limitations and our aspirations. Just keep in mind that the form guidance takes reflects more about the orientation of the person receiving it than about the guidance itself. What matters more than the form is the essence of the guidance, and the two should not be confused.

Because it is filtered through the beliefs and limitations of our personality, I believe that all information we receive from higher guidance gets unintentionally distorted in some way. Although an individual may truly be extending to a refined spiritual level and tapping a very high source, the process of bringing that information into form is like translating material from an unlimited language into a limited one. Something always gets lost in the translation. The material is first filtered (at least slightly) by the beliefs, needs, and experiences of the individual. Then it is filtered again by the beliefs, needs, and experiences of each person who hears or reads the information.

Many people are spiritually clear and open, yet even the most aware human beings are still in bodies. When there is an alive body, there is always a personality, and even the most enlightened personality carries some filters. As we continue to evolve, stretching our abilities to bring unlimited awareness through our personality, less and less distortion will appear. For the time being, simply be aware that no information credited to higher guidance conveys exactly and completely the truth that is intended.

How, then, can you know if information you receive, read, or hear from someone else will benefit you? By fine tuning your own intuition and listening to it. Intuition is the voice of your true self. Your true self will always recognize truth and let you know whether information is relevant for you. Remember, attunement to higher guidance is not meant to replace or invalidate your inner truth; it is meant to remind you of it. You are your greatest guide.

Part III
Self-Love

◆

Your Source of Life

10

The Love That You Are

Vibrant love is manifest in the bones, tissues, and physiology of your body. It is your essence, the seed energy for your emotions, thoughts, and awareness. No matter how complex, every element of your internal and external realities originates entirely from love. This love is the life force, the common denominator in all things and all beings. Through this life force you are one with everything and everyone in the world—and beyond.

Self-love is the experience of the love that you are. This love is a brilliant light. Like the sun or a star, it shines continuously in the core of your being, even when it is not seen or felt. When you have bouts of feeling unworthy, unlovable, resentful, or critical, the cloud cover of your personality has moved in and has blocked your experience of the light. But no matter what may prevent you from seeing the love that you are, the love is still there—always. As you learn self-love, you are simply learning to see through that cloud cover to the ever-shining light of your true being.

When you think about loving yourself, you may still be focused in the cloud cover. In trying to feel good about yourself, you may think, "I love myself because I am generous, sensitive, and have a loving heart. I care about people, and I am intelligent, and I really do look pretty good, and. . . ." Cherishing those traits in your personality is valuable, but that is not truly self-love. Learning to appreciate certain patterns within the cloud cover is not quite the same as breaking through it.

What is beneath the cloud cover does not need to be loved—because it is love itself. Living with self-love is accepting the love that is your essence. You can allow the warmth of that light to shine through and be with you in your daily life—

when you are alone, when you are quiet, even when you are in pain or under stress. Whether you feel joyous, loving, angry, or resentful does not matter. The love that you are is not dependent on how you feel or behave at the personality level. Its light penetrates all aspects of your being, and you can have it no matter how you feel.

You never have to "get over"
any of your other feelings
to find love.

If you are dealing with a deep, painful feeling and cannot seem to move through it, you can still draw on the healing power of self-love. Perhaps you are lost in anger; you have a shield of defensiveness around you, and from behind it you are shaking your fists in pain and rage. Even in the midst of that intensity, you can allow some of the warmth and vitality of the love that you are to seep through, to fill you alongside the frustration and anger.

You do not have to give up your anger, sadness, despair, or other feelings. Allow the love that you are to shine through and touch you along with your feelings. Then you are empowering yourself. You are allowing your humanness to be the vehicle for your unlimited essence, and your life is enriched.

11

Loving Yourself

Pay attention to how you love yourself. To the degree that you open to the love that you are, you can open fully to life around you and to the experiences you have come into the world to embrace.

There is no need to assess whether things are going well enough in your life for you to deserve to love yourself. The two are not related. You deserve to love yourself always, regardless of how well you seem to be doing in life, how successful you feel you are or are not, or how others feel about you.

The essence of who you are is unchanged by what you do and how you experience your life. Your essence is brilliance, love, and the vitality of life itself. And that is always worth loving. The difficulty comes in being able to know and trust that this very essence is indeed manifested in you in every moment, regardless of whether you or other people are able to perceive it on a regular basis. The essence is always there within you, and it is important to love yourself dearly for it.

Allow yourself to use your experiences as mirrors of learning. When you have the feeling in a relationship that the other person does not seem to love you enough or love you in the way that you want to be loved, stop for a moment and look at how you love yourself. Do you love yourself completely, without judgment and without limitation? Are you able to love yourself unconditionally, regardless of how others are seeing you and regardless of whether you are everything you want to be?

As you experience pain in not feeling
loved by another, know that you are also
feeling the loss and heartache
of not fully loving yourself.

In early childhood, many people are taught by family members and society to stop loving themselves fully. Infants and small children automatically love themselves and all beings they come into contact with: those in human form, those in animal form, and those in spirit form. Children's receptors are wide open. They receive all beings and love them all unconditionally; that is their natural state.

Yet by the age of two or so, many children have already learned to stop loving themselves completely and, therefore, have learned to stop loving others completely. The two go hand in hand. That initial loss of loving oneself is indeed the greatest pain one can experience. It is the loss of the joy of being openly and whole-heartedly present in the world. In one way or another, all pain in relationships can be traced to that loss of love for oneself, loss of that open-heartedness and the ability to share it with the world.

Each day as you go about your activities, you may want to stop several times and briefly check in with yourself. In whatever you are doing in the moment, ask, "Am I loving myself while I do this?" As you drive, think, "Am I loving myself as I drive?" When you are at work, think, "Am I loving myself as I work?" When you are speaking with someone, eating a meal, having an argument, taking a bath, or making love, ask, "Am I loving myself in this moment?"

This questioning allows you to begin to notice how you feel about yourself and how automatically you forget, over and over, the love that you are. It also allows you to consciously use each activity as an opportunity to open to greater self-love. It's to your advantage to learn to love yourself continuously, even when—or perhaps especially when—you are engaged in something that is unpleasant or mundane to you. Being able to love yourself in this continuous way will assist you in opening to greater realms of awareness, both within yourself and in the world around you.

12

Letting Love Light Your Life

When you are not in loving alignment with yourself, it's as though there is always a war going on between you and the world, one which can never quite be healed. Or you may sense a perpetual emptiness, an inner gap that you can never seem to fill. But when your energy is deeply aligned in self-love, the power of love radiates out from your being and transforms the quality of your life.

To envision this, let's take an imaginary journey.

◆

Meditation
Letting Love Light Your Life

To begin, gently allow your awareness to move into your heart center, wherever it seems to be in your chest. Imagine that no matter what tension or restriction you may feel in your body, your heart center is opening and coming to life. It's as though the heart center itself is breathing and radiating a beautiful vibration of love that you have never before experienced.

This vibration of love is so powerful and carries so much of the essence of life that nothing diminishes it. No matter what else you experience, this deep vibration of love is constant. With each breath you take, this love becomes brighter and more alive within you. Give yourself a few moments to receive this gift of love as it streams throughout your body.

As you continue to allow this feeling of love to be present in the heart of your being, imagine for a moment what it would be like if this love were to radiate outward into your auric field, the energy sphere surrounding your body. Your body and the space around your body would be bathed in this feeling of love.

Remember that this love is not diminished by anything you can say or do or think. Nothing can take this love from you. It is as powerful as the life force itself, and it continues to fill your body and auric field no matter what other thoughts you think or challenges you meet. Imagine what it would feel like to go through your life with this continuous love surrounding you.

Now imagine what it would be like if this love not only filled your heart, your body, and your auric field but radiated outward into your world—filling your house, your workplace, your town, spreading across the planet. Everything in your world would be bathed with this love.

You can imagine, then, that everywhere you go you would encounter love. All people and all places would be bathed with this love. Every time you had a conversation with someone, you would see and feel this love. And nothing anyone could say, do, think, or feel would diminish this powerful vibration.

This means that every situation you encountered, no matter how sad or worrisome or painful, would always carry the energy of love with it. So if something should happen to upset you, you would also feel love; the love would be there alongside the upset feeling. And, of course, when you were happy you would feel love with the happiness. Imagine what a difference it would make! It would mean that nothing in your life would ever come to you that did not come with love. Every experience would carry with it the vibration of the very love that emanates from your heart center. What a powerful thought!

———————————————— ◆ ————————————————

And it is a powerful reality. It is already taking place in your life this very moment and will continue to take place every day. It is already real. You have simply not noticed it most of the time. Before you took these moments to focus on the feeling of love in your heart, you were not so aware of it. Similarly, you have been not so aware of the love that is permeating all of physical reality. The love has been there all along. When you do notice this love, it is a great joy. This experience need not be rare; the way to create a more constant experience of this love is simply to open to it, moment by moment.

Allow yourself to want to experience the true light and love that you are, and remember that desire often. That desire takes place at a very deep level and can affect the day-by-day creation of your life. The power of such a true desire can assist you in opening your heart and remembering the love that is your source of life.

13

Choosing Love

Your mighty ally in opening to greater self-love is your intention. This ally will gladly serve you as you start each day, but you must give it direction. As you get up in the morning and your feet touch the floor, you can pause for a moment and say, "To the depth of my being, more than anything else today, I choose to experience the love that I am." You may also choose to remember that phrase from time to time throughout the day. With such clear intention, all experiences of that day will be aligned toward expanding your self-love.

Of course, calling on your ally does not necessarily mean that only pleasant things will happen to you that day. It simply means that whatever does happen—whether you like it or not, whether it is comfortable or uncomfortable—will serve the purpose of bringing you into greater self-love. Naturally you will have some experiences in life that feel painful or uncomfortable. But when you have aligned with the purpose of embodying greater love, even those difficult times will, in the end, bring you that love.

You hold yourself back when you say, "I want more love in my life, but I am not willing to go through difficult experiences to get it. I only want pleasant experiences." That limits you. Love is present everywhere, and to embody complete love of self, you will be put to the challenge of taking in a full range of life's experiences.

Being willing to open
to total love
means being willing
to open to all of life.

Sometimes growth into love takes place at an unconscious level, and you do not see evidence of it right away. You may not always consciously know when an experience, either pleasant or unpleasant, has just opened you to greater love. It may take time as the new experience of love works its way outward from the deep subtle energy within toward the denser level of sensation that can be felt in a conscious way. New patterns begin long before you can feel or see them; you do not have control over the process of love's emergence.

Have faith. As you repeat your intention to open to more self-love, you can trust that the work will be done. Your learning will be guided by the very source of love deep within your being that you are calling forth into your life. You cannot have a more trustworthy guide. Every situation and experience will automatically be fertile ground for the growth of this love. In doubtful moments, it may strengthen your trust to remind yourself of your commitment: "I want greater love in my life. I open to greater self-love, and I willingly receive the experiences that can bring this to me."

14

Loving Others

Loving yourself increases your love of others. You may have been taught to skip loving yourself and go straight to loving other people, as though it is "right" or "good" to love others more than yourself. Ironically, it is impossible to be successful at this effort. Love of others cannot truly be learned or experienced unless there is already love of self.

Self-love is the basic pool you draw from for all other forms of love. When you allow yourself to be bathed with the love that you are, your being energetically emanates the vibration of love into the world. Self-love is what gives you the very ability to experience love for other people.

> *Your capacity for love of others*
> *naturally deepens*
> *as your love of self grows.*

Put another way, when you are able to know and love yourself, you spontaneously gain the ability to know and love all beings around you. Whatever difficulty you have remembering to see others in their essence is a reflection of the difficulty you have seeing your own essence. So when you want to love others more, when you wish that your heart could be bigger and your judgments less quick or less harsh, remember that what you really want is to be more in touch with the essence of your own being. You need to open your heart more to yourself. Nourish yourself first with your love, and that love will grow outward.

When you insist on seeing or loving others more fully than you do yourself, it is a tremendous strain. It means that your outer relationships must be lived in a way that you are not living inside. You must keep giving to others what you are not giving to yourself. If you are not loving yourself, it takes exhaustive energy to love others, and you must be vigilant at it. Because that love is based on effort rather than on natural emanation, you cannot stop trying to love for a moment or the loving will stop. But when you truly love yourself, love for others follows in a way that is continuous, natural, and effortless. Then your life is blessed, and your love is the blessing you share with the world.

15

Recognizing True Love

Relationships with other people can be complex. You often have to assess others' intentions. "Is this person honest with me?" "Is it safe for me to be close with this person?" "Does this person really love me or have my best interests at heart?" How can you judge these things accurately? You may sometimes feel at risk for being fooled, disappointed, or hurt.

When love of self is real to you, you are less frequently deceived by others. It becomes more clear when others are (and are not) operating from a place of love and honor. By carrying the energy pattern of love within you, you will automatically be able to recognize a matching reality in others.

It's when you are unfamiliar with self-love that you genuinely need to be protective. Without love of self, you do not carry the energy pattern of true love within your conscious experience, so you don't have a reliable standard by which to assess other people. In such situations, realize the limitation you are working with; then turn your focus around and open to loving yourself. Say, "I open to deep self-love I know I can trust." Empower yourself. In the long run, self-love will bring you the love you want from others as well as the ability to recognize that love.

16

Love and Physical Reality

Some people pass through a phase in their spiritual growth of holding a critical view of the physical realm, and they extend this criticism to themselves and others for being in physical form. They may complain that spiritual growth is slow in physical form and that physical reality itself is dense and limited. In short, they feel that the physical realm is an inferior place to be. They may even suggest that the only beings who live in physical reality are the ones who cannot "make it" in the higher realms, those who have not grown enough to leave physical form once and for all.

This viewpoint is usually a reflection of the personality's unloving judgment of self. Unlimited spirit tends to carry a different view, one in which no reality is perceived as better or worse than another.

Physical reality is a magnificent reality,
in spite of how limited it feels.

Many beings of pure light and love choose to incarnate into the physical realm because it holds such rich experience and challenge. When such beings come into physical form, they open to experiences at the physical level for the purpose of divine growth. That growth is about learning to find love even in the seeming density and limitation that characterize physical reality.

It is out of love for yourself that you have chosen to come into physical form. And it is out of that same love of self that you continue to be here, researching, experiencing, creating, experimenting. Likewise, when you leave physical reality, it will be out of love of self that you move on when you are ready. Whenever you move from one form of reality to another, the motivation for the leap always comes from love of self. Love is the fuel, the power that moves you from one realm to another. So the fact that you are here in physical reality at all is proof that you have loved yourself enough to make the journey. The trick now is to continue loving yourself while you are here.

The only true injury in life occurs
by going into an experience
and not being able to find the love in it.

Part of the journey you are making through physical reality involves learning to find love in the midst of every situation, every feeling, and every belief you encounter. For example, grief or loss is an intense, often unbearable emotion. Yet, as you allow yourself to surrender deeply to that very human feeling, at the core of it you will come upon a ray of light that is love, and that will be the healer. It will not take away the pain. It may not even take away the feeling of loss, but it will transform it. And it will mean that the feeling of loss or grief can no longer deny you the experience of love.

Love and life are one and the same. Vibrationally, love is the very substance of life. No wonder it is so frightening to be out of touch with love—that means being out of touch with life and the being that you truly are. You may fear criticism because you fear not loving yourself. You may fear your anger because you fear not being able to love others. When love is fragile and elusive, fear arises in many forms. But as you increase your ability to experience the love that is at the core of every feeling, you will find less and less in life to fear.

Attunement
Self-Love #1

Three times a day, stop for one to five minutes to align with the deep love radiating from your being. If you are sitting, sit with the awareness that you are opening your heart to the pure love and light and creative life force that you are. Feel or sense that love filling you and radiating outward. While you are driving, drive with the awareness that you are making that same deep connection. If you are talking to someone, be aware that as you talk you are also opening to that deep inner source of love. As this love fills you, it weaves itself into your daily life.

Attunement
Self-Love #2

When you are in bed at night waiting for sleep, simply feel or sense the love that emanates deep within your heart center. If you use words, just use them long enough to get in touch with the feeling of the love that you are. You might gently speak or think, "I align with the love that I am" or "The true love and light of my being radiates through me." Allow yourself to feel that love and light, however slight it may be. Focus on that feeling, letting it grow as it moves you into sleep.

Part IV

Journey into Form

---◆---

The Exploration of Limitation

17

The Journey So Far

Your journey into this life began in a state of pure spirit and unlimited being. Before coming into physical form, your experience was not restricted by time or limited to sequential events. You lived in a fluidity and a unity in which literally all things were possible. Although you knew individuality, there was no separation between one being and another or between one thing and another. Everything and everyone were recognized as expressions of your expanded being.

As unlimited spirit, you were a master of creation. The very instant you thought a thought, the appropriate form to express it was manifested. The very instant you felt a desire, that desire (or perhaps its fulfillment) was manifested. All your inner experience and refined emotion naturally materialized into form so you could observe it or interact with it.

You lived in a highly creative state. No thought was just a thought, no feeling just a feeling. Every experience was an impulse of creative force. Because you were not in a physical body or in physical reality, all forms were more subtle, more fluid than anything physical. Yet they were real. And because your awareness was not limited by form, you were conscious at all levels. You never forgot that the manifestations you witnessed and interacted with flowed from your own creative source.

Could it be that all these characteristics are also true about physical reality? Think about them: unity, fluidity of time, instant manifestation, malleable form, all experience as creative impulse, unlimited possibilities, multilevel awareness. Your sense of life in physical form may tell you that these things are possibly true about the physical realm, but within certain limits. This is because your experience of physical reality is based on limitation.

All the characteristics listed (and many more) are true of the unlimited realm without any limits applied to them whatsoever. Your experience in that realm took place at a very refined level, and the deep, distant memory of it is guiding you in this lifetime. For example, you may be frustrated in this lifetime that the things you want to manifest seem to take so long to come into physical form. This slowness of physical reality contrasts with a faint memory of the tremendous speed of manifesting in the unlimited realm.

In physical reality, there is a tendency
to be hypnotized by solid matter.

What seems most solid, most unbudgeable, seems most real. You define and direct your life within the constraints you observe and choose to believe in. Because the range of your experience and action is determined by what you think is possible, impossibility actually shapes your reality. It is impossibility that tells you what the limits to physical life are and where you can expect to find them.

Your personality is the aspect of your being that has adapted to physical reality. It listens to limitation and impossibility, believes what they say, and sees to it that you live according to their restrictions. You can be happy, but only to a point. You can be magical and creative, but only to a point. You can have what you want and need, but only to a point. You can break through any barrier in life, but. . . . Your personality's basic job is to control your unlimitedness and act as your navigator through the limited realm of physical form.

Living in physical reality
is a much more dense experience
than living in unlimited spirit
—until you realize that even in physical
form, unlimited spirit is with you.

Unlimited spirit is within the nature of your being. It came with you into your body, and you have access to it whenever you choose to open to it. You may ask, "If unlimitedness is so close at hand, then why do I feel slowed down and limited by physical reality? Why does my personality seem so much more real than my spirit does? Why can't I seem to live in unlimited awareness on a daily basis?"

Coming into this lifetime was a process of adjusting your awareness from the realm of spirit to the realm of physical form. Whenever you move from the unlimitedness of spirit into a new realm, part of the adjustment involves acclimating to the prevailing consciousness of the new realm. As you moved into physical reality at the beginning of this lifetime, you took on the consciousness that was active in the physical realm when you came in. Because you came into physical form at a time when the overall consciousness of those already here was one of separation and limitation, you took on separation and limitation as your new reality to explore.

You did this in two ways: first by simply slipping into a physical body and then by being receptive to personal and cultural conditioning.

How can moving into a body affect your consciousness? The physical body is a marvelous instrument. It quite literally allows you to be here, yet it is more than just a physical container. The body is made so that its vibrations precisely match the vibrations of consciousness prevailing on the physical plane. This means that your body's job is to hold your being's vibration within a certain range that exactly reflects the vibrational range of physical reality and the collective physical consciousness.

The body also exactly matches the vibration, or energy pattern, of the physical earth. You absorb energy from the earth with every step you take, and that energy keeps reminding your body of the proper vibration for holding your spirit's focus here. You have energy receptors, especially in your hands and feet, for making contact with the earth and for receiving its energy patterns. This energy nurtures your body and keeps it in vibrational synch with the earth and with physical reality.

When you became physical, your consciousness was also bombarded with mental, emotional, and experiential conditioning. You grew up in a culture that reflected to you, over and over, information and instruction about the reality of the collective consciousness of the physical plane. As you took in this information you were pressured to adopt it as your operative reality so you could be more fully present and active in the physical realm.

For example, most people had the experience of growing up in families in which they were not seen and honored for all of who they truly were. As infants, they were not perceived as wise and ancient beings whose unlimited spirits extended far beyond their small bodies. In early childhood, they were not recognized as being completely aware and sensitive to the thoughts, feelings, and energies moving from person to person around them. In midchildhood, their ability to draw on memory of unlimited being was dismissed or overlooked by people closest to them.

Instead, most children were viewed through a projection of the consciousness from which the family was already operating. Members of the family were no longer living from expanded consciousness and a state of unity. Their experience of unlimited spirit had been dulled and replaced by the more limited reality of the personality, which is based on separation. Having forgotten their unity, these individuals saw themselves as completely separate from others rather than deeply connected to them. Having forgotten that all things are truly possible, they experienced life as a struggle against difficult odds.

So the family related from the personality and projected that reality onto the children, seeing and relating to them as personalities, also separate and limited. In response, the children learned to experience themselves as alone, no longer one with others in a deeply spiritual way and no longer one with their own unlimited being.

It is painful for children to realize (often even in infancy) that they are not recognized for who they truly are and that, to maintain the connection and intimacy they need from the people around them, they must forget their inner truth. Their inner senses tell them, "I have come here to connect with people. For that to happen, we must share some common reality. The unlimited aspect of my nature is not real to people here, so I must set it aside. I must take on an identity that is real to my family, my schoolmates, my teachers, and the other people I depend on. Because I do not appear real to them as I truly am in the fullness of my spirit, I will become whatever they can relate to."

Most children allow themselves to be molded to the cultural consciousness to achieve the human bonding they need.

The cost to the children is that bit by bit, year by year, the rigidity of the personality is reinforced and more of their true being is put aside, lost in the adjustment. When these children grow older and have more thoroughly forgotten the expanded levels of their being, they then play out the other side of that dynamic. They become the adults who unconsciously encourage the new children to put aside their unlimitedness. These acculturated adults no longer recognize the essence of unlimited children as real.

Very few parents realize that they do this with their children. Their experience is that they love their children and want to connect with them. They are simply unaware that they have already put much of themselves aside and are, therefore, missing much of who their children are. They are unaware of the

pressure this puts on their children, and, through that uncon-
sciousness, they perpetuate the pattern. None of this is done
with malice or with conscious intent, yet it is a chain reaction
that has gone from generation to generation for centuries.

Something unique is happening in our culture at this time.
The chain reaction is slowing. The pattern of passing on an
inheritance of limited consciousness is transforming into a pattern of passing on continuous expanding awareness.

This generation and the next three or four generations will
be extremely active in supporting the new pattern. In fact,
people who hear or read these words are already involved in
this transformation. We do this work by reclaiming the lost
essence of our own being, by coming Home to true self. As we
live from true self, we recognize the true self in others and create an environment in which unlimited spirit can flourish in
everyone's life.

True self is your link
between personality and unlimited being.

Your personality has become acclimated to the limited
consciousness of physical form and accepts it as reality. Unlimited being is the state of pure spirit you have come from. It
is time for the two to merge. Because true self is based in pure
spirit and is conscious (and loving!) of your personality, it
embraces both realities and holds the space for their union.

18

Illusion and Truth

At first glance it may appear that life in the physical realm is too
limited to enable you to bring truly unlimited being into your

life. Even if you long for greater awareness, your experience in the physical world may tell you that a limited reality is reluctant to make room for an unlimited one. The container of form and personality may feel too small, too tight, or too dense to hold the expansiveness of spirit for very long. Your personality will affirm this and will tell you that limitation is a barrier to unlimitedness. But really, the opposite is true: unlimitedness frees limitation.

All limitation in physical reality is illusion.

As long as you believe that any limitation is real, you will experience it as real and will find much data to back up that "fact." Limitation can be very convincing. It can look real, feel real, and act real. But as you open your heart and your higher centers and are willing to let expanded experience be real in your world, limitation weakens and gives way.

Limitation is no match for unlimited being. Limitation is real as long as you believe in it and interpret it as a force that holds you back. This is something your personality does on a daily basis. However, limitation dissolves the moment it is met with unlimitedness.

Noticing your tendency toward limitation can be frustrating. Yet even if you are frustrated about the limitations in your life, there is no need to resist or fight them. Fighting your limitations is simply engaging one illusion with a second illusion: that you can fight or dominate the first one. The way to regain your connection with true self and reclaim the unlimitedness of your being is not to go through your life attacking your limitations. It is to allow unlimited being to come into your life alongside those limitations.

Unlimitedness is the greater truth.

Unlimitedness is the truth that brought you forth into this life; it is the truth that maintains your presence in this life; and it is the truth that will go with you as you leave this life. Illusion dissolves whenever it is met with truth.

Bringing in unlimited awareness alongside an experience of limitation will catalyze natural transformation. Because unlimitedness carries greater essential truth than does limitation, unlimited experience has a magnetic-like pull that prompts limitation to restructure. Prompted by this force, limited experience will restructure itself energetically into a pattern that matches—or becomes—the unlimited experience. Simply put, limitation will shift to accommodate, and ultimately support, unlimitedness as the dominant reality.

As this happens there is a merging of energies. The energy that previously went into maintaining the illusion of limitation, as well as the energy that went into fighting or resisting that limitation, is then used to support the greater experience of unlimited being. In a sense, it is a process of energetically ingesting the karma (or limitation) of your life, digesting it with the greatness of your being, and then allowing it to become fuel to propel you forward into more profound experiences of unlimited consciousness.

19

Living a Split

The essence of spirit is unlimited love and compassion. All spiritual sight is sight with love. All spiritual thought is thought with love. All spiritual sense or feeling is with love as well. There is no experience of a truly spiritual nature that does not come through love. The personality, however, does not always feel love, for that is not necessarily the personality's job. The personality's job is to explore the experience of limitation.

All thoughts or feelings that limit you come from your personality, as do all perceptions or assumptions that anything is impossible. According to your personality's perspective, successful living means knowing the limitations of yourself, others, and the world and focusing your creative efforts within those confines.

In your personality's experience, there are limits to everything, including the amount and conditions of love available within yourself, others, and the world. Because of this apparently limited supply of love, your personality is prone to being separated from love easily, often simply by the words or actions of other people. So it makes judgments, holds grudges, and harbors resentment. In that state of alienation from the unlimited love of true self, it is lost in its own reality.

Rest assured that the essence of your being is not formed or changed by the limitations of your personality. Unlimited love, unlimited wisdom, and unlimited creativity continue to be your true state. From this essence all elements of your life, including your personality, are designed to give your soul the greatest opportunity for compassionate learning. Your guide through this learning is your true self.

Why does your guide seem so elusive? Your true self is fully conscious of itself and of the totality of your being, including your personality. Yet your personality is not very conscious of true self because your personality's reality does not include true self.

Since your identity in the physical realm is with your personality, your personality's reality is most real to you in your everyday life. Your conscious awareness may occasionally open to the expansiveness of true self and spirit, but it usually snaps back like a rubber band to the limitation of personality.

Because you experience these two realities as separate rather than integrated, it is as though you are living a split.

True self is continuously present.
It communicates with you at all times
but speaks in a very refined voice.

Because you turned your ear away from true self to adapt to the physical realm, you are no longer so consciously attuned to its frequency. Personality is aligned with denser experience, and you are accustomed to personality's louder, more obvious voice. It tells you that whatever is loudest, densest, and most obvious is most real. In contrast, true self's voice is like a faint whisper and speaks through subtlety and refined experience. Often, you do not recognize it.

You may be entering a phase in your life when your orientation to the two seemingly separate realities of personality and true self is shifting. The more subtle experiences are now emerging as real. True self has always been more closely aligned with the truth of your being than has personality, but now you are developing the ability to listen to true self and take action based on its guidance. True self's whispers are heard through your intuition, and action taken from this source changes your life.

Personality has become quite well developed in the current culture. This maturity brings us to the brink of expansion into a new identity. We have gone as far as we can go by identifying so strongly with personality. We have lived the reality of personality so fully that we have completed that cycle of evolution and are now ready to move on. In fact, for survival we *must* move on to greater awareness. Because of its basis in limitation, personality has created so much dilemma and distress, at the global level as well as in our individual lives, that we must make the shift to true self to realize solutions. We need to draw from a more expanded and creative perspective to meet our challenges.

This need is no accident. Whenever a collective consciousness completes its "study" of a particular level of awareness, it finds itself somewhat off-balance. This is natural and guarantees a built-in momentum and motivation for breaking through into the next reality to be explored. The natural state of imbalance brought on by having so fully identified with personality now pushes us forward into a new identity, collectively and individually.

This identity comprises a merging of the two identities we have been ricocheting between. As this merging progresses, we will feel less and less forced to choose between limitation and unlimitedness; they will no longer be like oil and water, but together will become a new substance.

Understand that in this process neither reality wins over the other, and neither reality loses any of its characteristics. Unlimitedness is simply brought into limitation, which means that in your life, your spirit becomes integrated into your personality on a conscious, everyday basis.

Many people still think that being on a spiritual path means fighting the personality and that enlightenment means defeating the personality once and for all, as though the spirit is somehow set free in that "victory." But, in truth, the spirit has never been imprisoned by the personality, not even for a moment. (Unlimitedness is never truly limited by anything, not even by the greatest limitation.) The spirit has only loved the personality, endlessly bathing it—as it bathes everything—in the light of unlimitedness.

If you want to be enlightened,
be just that: in light. Shine the light
of love and acceptance into every part
of your being, as you already are.

Cherish your personality. You do not always have to identify with it or be restricted by its limited awareness, but honor it as an expression of your creative life force. Your personality has done an excellent job of showing you the reality of limitation and is worthy of your light.

Cherishing your personality will be difficult if you feel that it controls you. If you feel that your personality keeps you from greater spiritual awareness, you will have a tendency to take a battle stance and fight for its defeat. This position puts you at a decided disadvantage. You can never really win this battle, so the struggle can go on and on for lifetimes. It will not be resolved until you give up and allow something new to happen.

Sometimes it does feel as though your personality's limitations control you and that if only you could rid yourself of your personality—or wall yourself off from it—you would be free to soar the spiritual heights you deeply remember. It may feel that way, but feeling is not always what is most true.

Your personality does not control you; you identify with it. That is an important distinction. As you grew up and "forgot" true self to fit in with the consciousness that surrounded you, you chose to identify with personality as the dominant reality. It was choice. And it is still choice.

The reason why this distinction is so important is that whatever you choose to identify with is what will be most real. You make your personality's reality real in your life by choosing it. If you choose to keep identifying with personality, limitation and separation will continue to be the building materials of all situations and experiences in your life.

There is nothing wrong with identifying with personality; it is genuinely a fine way to live. Limitation is as divine as unlimitedness. If, however, you are uncomfortable with the confines of limitation and find yourself yearning for more expansive experiences, you can choose to identify with unlimitedness as well. Choosing is done over and over in your everyday life; each issue you face brings you the opportunity to make a conscious and sincere choice to align with true self.

Everything in this book is about inviting unlimitedness to be real in your life. It can be used as a manual for reminding yourself to be purposeful—and creative—about directing your intention and choosing your reality.

20

Choosing Your Reality

The new reality is the merging of unlimitedness into limitation, formlessness into the realm of form. What will it mean for you personally? For the planet as a whole? The way to find out is to keep living and paying attention.

All people are preparing, consciously or unconsciously, for dramatic changes in their lives. For some the change may come slowly and for others quickly, but for everyone it is dramatic change. No one on the planet is free from this change because, quite literally, the entire consciousness of the planet is making the shift.

> *Your consciousness*
> *is manifested externally*
> *in your life.*

As your consciousness shifts, the external manifestations and experiences in your life that were created from your old consciousness will restructure to catch up. This is something you have no choice about at the personality level. Your spirit has already chosen to put you here to participate in this collective transformation, and your true self is already guiding you through the life changes that come with this expansion and growth.

Your challenge during these changes is to allow yourself to shift intuitively into a more refined sight, a more refined hearing, a more refined sense of self. From there you will naturally live with a more refined perception of the world around you. You will be in synch with the change.

Your attunement to the truth of your being is increasing. As you allow yourself to listen to it, to see from it, and to be in alignment with it, the challenges you face in your life will support your transformation.

To the degree that your personality resists your transformation, you will have difficulty. Understand that there is nothing wrong with this resistance; resistance is part of personality's expression. You do not need to fear your difficulties; they will not defeat you and do not necessarily mean you are off track. They are simply reflections of your inner struggle. Use those reflections as reminders to be patient and caring with yourself.

Just as there is no value in fighting the illusion of limitation, there is no value in fighting personality's resistance. You can, however, benefit by allowing personality its struggle and by extending compassion to it. Alongside personality's struggle, open your awareness to true self and invite that refined sense of unlimited being into your life. Place it next to the struggle, and allow true self to energetically soothe the fears, the doubts, the uncertainties of personality.

In other words, live the split. Allow yourself to be aware of both the limited and unlimited aspects of your being. Recognize personality's familiar thoughts and feelings, its old ways of being. Notice its fears and resistance to your movement into the new reality. From there, gently open to true self by sensing its guidance, compassion, expanded sight, and unlimited being.

At times you will be particularly aware that you have conscious choice about whether to identify with and act from personality's reality or from that of true self. Experiment with choosing true self whenever you can.

*Each time you let true self
guide your actions, you strengthen
your ability to live in unlimitedness.*

Yet, there may still be times when you do not seem to be quite ready or able to act from true self. Instead, you catch yourself automatically proceeding from the habituated responses and beliefs of personality. That is all right, too. Just be conscious about it. Be honest with yourself about what you are doing; staying aware allows new growth to come to you in those situations. Then acknowledge that true self is there, patiently and compassionately waiting for the time when you can allow it to be of greater service.

The transition from personality to true self is progressive rather than sudden, a weave rather than a sharp cut. You have unlimited freedom to allow your own pattern and pace of growth to emerge. Don't worry if your growth doesn't seem to be fast enough. There will be numerous opportunities to choose your way and to strengthen your choice. You are supported in this process more than you know.

21

Emanations of Light

You are connected at a deeply spiritual level to all other people who share your desire for greater personal growth and spiritual exploration. You are also connected to a very wise and loving collective of nonphysical spirit beings who assist you in your growth. In fact, you are recognized, loved, and supported, in the totality of your being, by an unlimited number of beings of light and love in every moment. These beings are in a state of absolute alignment with the source of all life. They have no limit in their access to expanded consciousness and no limit in their ability to radiate that consciousness to others.

When beings are in this state of alignment, their energy is automatically available to all who aspire toward unlimited awareness. These fully aligned beings never tire of giving. Giving is their joy, their natural reality.

Just as water experiences
no effort or fatigue in flowing,
beings of light and love
do not tire from their giving to you.

These beings completely support you in your spiritual transformation and are continuously emanating waves of light to the collective consciousness of our planet. These waves of light carry energy patterns that exactly mirror the energy patterns of your own higher consciousness. Your true self recognizes these waves for what they are and receives them, allowing your whole being to be reminded at a deep level of your unlimited nature.

It is by choice that you accept these emanations. People who are genuinely not interested in remembering the totality of their being in this lifetime will ignore these waves of light and will not receive them. They will simply go about living their lives in whatever other ways they have set up for their greatest growth. However, most people are, at the essence level, quite interested in standing up and receiving these emanations. You may even sense that your own longing for expanded awareness is so strong that not only are you standing up, but you are waving your arms and shouting, "Over here! I'll take more light! Over here!" Your spiritual enthusiasm is shared by countless others.

As each wave of light is received within the group consciousness, it generates a pull on the source so that the next wave of light is then released. When that wave is received, it also generates a pull for the next one, and so on. This creates a natural flow of waves of light, each bringing with it a more accelerated consciousness. Because each wave must be fully received before it exerts a pull on the next one to be released, the flow can never out-pace your ability to assimilate the light into your life. The flow is in harmony with you and cannot stimulate growth too quickly or too slowly.

As you receive this energy and allow yourself to be bathed in it, you automatically begin to radiate it outward into your life. Released into your life, this energy creates experiences that remind you, at a conscious level, of who you truly are.

Many of your beliefs about yourself as well as outer situations in your life may have been created from identifying with your "not true self" and could be interfering with your having a more conscious awareness of unlimited being. As you continue to identify with these beliefs and situations, usually unconsciously, they can act like physical, emotional, or spiritual blocks that keep you feeling stuck or unable to live out your true potential. When you are ready, the radiance of light and love streaming through your being will enliven these blocks, sometimes causing them to seem even more powerful. Yet, as you allow yourself to experience and move through these blocks, they will be transformed into energy that ultimately supports you in being who you truly are.

This inner transformation will bring change into your outer life to the degree that you need it. If the foundation of your life has been based on who you thought you should be or on other people's images of you, rather than on who you essentially are, then your whole life will change. Although such deep change can be difficult, painful, or frightening at times, it always leads, at the guidance of your spirit, to your greater fulfillment.

In this transition you may have the feeling that some (or all) of the structures in your life are collapsing: your work, your primary relationship, your friendships, your basic view of self and the world. There are often feelings of loss, fear, despair, helplessness, and failure that go with this change. From the perspective of the soul, however, there is no such thing as failure, there is no such thing as loss. Your life will be reconstructed by your own greater self, this time reflecting who you are instead of who you are not. That is the stability beneath the change.

When you have a life that is based
on who you truly are,
no amount of change can shake you,
no amount of uncertainty
can bring instability.

Your stability is no longer based on holding onto things in a static form and trying to keep change from occurring. Instead, you have a greater strength that comes from being able to live from your true self no matter what is changing around you.

Throughout this transition, the beings of light and love who joyfully emanate the waves of expanded consciousness to the planet are available to you. All your thoughts, feelings, and actions that carry an intent toward greater spiritual growth are automatically supported and reinforced by these beings. You can draw upon their assistance and guidance whenever you desire it.

You may tend to underestimate the power in your desire for personal assistance. Every true desire or request from the heart is received instantly, and assistance is always given. Always. When a genuine plea for greater growth goes out, beings who have already achieved that level, so to speak, automatically respond and come forward to assist.

Assistance and guidance are given to you through the experiences of your life. Assistance may come to you in the forms in which you are requesting or expecting it. Or it may come to you in altogether different forms, through a set of experiences you would not have thought to ask for. You can never know for sure what forms (or timing) the assistance will take, but it will always be according to what serves your greater purpose.

Keep in mind that in reaching "outward" to higher guidance, you are also, naturally and automatically, reaching inward to the higher levels of your being. In this way, as you ask for spirit assistance, you simultaneously align with your inner guidance. The source of your assistance only appears to be external.

Outer spirit guidance serves
as training wheels
for your awareness;
your own unlimited being
is the true vehicle
that propels you forward.

The miracle is that as beings of light and love become more real to you, you become more real to yourself. In opening to unlimited beings, you open to your own true self and bring empowerment into your life. Your true state of unity emerges, and you become aligned with the world around you. Although you are no longer lost to physical reality, you are no longer separate from any of it, either. Anyone who had previously seemed to be an adversary is no longer so, but is a companion.

Whatever had previously seemed to be an overwhelming difficulty now seems to be simply another way of receiving the vitality of life.

When this experience is real and grounded within you, you are so connected to your true self that you are connected to all things and all beings. There is nothing and no one that is not you. And making a change in your world is as simple as making a change in yourself.

Part V

Creating Your World

---◆---

Abundance and Manifesting

22

Longing for Abundance

Satisfying the longing for abundance begins by compassionately hearing your own long-muffled cries for greater self-love. It requires opening your heart to a level of inner need you may have ignored since childhood.

Being without self-love creates an inner barrenness, which manifests circumstances of lack in your outer life. If your inner experience is "I cannot have love of self; I cannot have the inner richness of fully being and loving all of who I am," then the outer experience will be "I cannot have the richness of what I most want in external reality, either." So you are likely to manifest recurring situations of not having enough money or love or friendship or whatever would bring a greater richness to your life.

To heal this empty spot, you must look within. Looking within does not mean being critical or coldly trying to track down your flaws to get rid of them, for harshness does not heal. Instead gently turn on an inner light, and look with tenderness and compassion to see how you can love yourself more.

Pretend for a moment that a small child whom you deeply love comes to you, crying, and sits on your lap. And pretend that you can see right away that this child's problem is self-esteem, that this child does not believe that she or he is really lovable. What would you do? You would not chastise this child for being so unself-loving. Instead, you would hold this child close and say, "I see that you have forgotten what a wonderful being you are. You have forgotten your beauty. You have forgotten your vitality, your magic, your lovability. I allow my love for who you are to fill you, to teach you, to remind you. I hold you

63

in this knowing of who you are so that you may remember to treasure and love yourself."

Do the same for yourself. Be willing to hold yourself on your lap, so to speak, and look into the being that you are with that same love and compassion. Simply see where you have forgotten your own magic, where you have forgotten the love that you are and the beauty you carry within. Then make a commitment to rediscover it in some way each day.

23

Receiving Abundance

Abundance is a given in your life, but you may not know it. You may feel removed from abundance and assume it exists somewhere "out there," perhaps for other people, perhaps as something you are trying to create or attain, something you are trying to break through to.

But you do not create abundance. You do not go out and get abundance. Abundance simply is. It is unchanging; like the sun it is always there. When you want the sun, you do not try to create it or control it. You simply step out into it and allow yourself to feel it. The same is true of abundance. Until now you may have spent your time standing in the shade, looking around and wondering, "Where's the abundance? It should be here soon. I'm working hard for it; where is it?"

It may be time to take some steps out of the shade and into the light where you can finally receive the abundance you have been longing for.

◆

Attunement
Receiving Abundance

1. Want.

Allow yourself to feel your desire fully. You may feel defeated at the prospect of feeling your desire without knowing for sure that it will be fulfilled. If your response to that feeling of defeat is to stop wanting, you are also stopping the energy of manifestation. You can proceed no further without reclaiming this vital energy of wanting. Fully allow all your true desires to come forward, regardless of whether they seem feasible or likely ever to be manifested.

There is a correlation between the degree to which you allow yourself to want and the degree to which you allow yourself to have. When you honestly allow the desire to grow as large as the desire itself wants to grow, you are more likely to allow the manifestation of its fulfillment. When you open the channel of creativity on the wanting end, it will open naturally at the manifesting end as well.

2. Feel.

When desires begin to be felt fully, other feelings may surface, too. Allow yourself to feel them. Sometimes it will be sadness or despair. "I want this for myself, and wanting makes me feel sad for all the times that I have not had it." "I feel the barrenness in my life, of what I have been missing for so long." "It feels futile. I don't know how to get what I want, and I probably can't have it anyway." There may also be anger. "Why didn't I let myself have this sooner? I am so angry to have lived my life in this way!" It is important that you allow such feelings—and others—to come forward and be felt. Let them grow to their own true size and be expressed.

3. Move.

Let your body move in action with these feelings. If the impulse is to throw yourself down and cry or wail like a child who is angry and frustrated and so very sad, give yourself permission to do that. Find a good support person to be with you if you need one, but allow your body its expression.

What is important here is letting your feelings move through in a healthy way. The physical body is the home of emotions; it is where they live. All emotions have physical, chemical and cellular effect. It is important to allow the motion of the emotions to go through the body so you can be clear, integrated, and open to new experience at all levels.

4. Trust.

Trust yourself. Trust the desires you have had, trust the feelings you have had in response, and trust the movement that has taken place. It has been real, it has been you, it has been important.

This step is a way of staying with yourself through thick and thin, regardless of how it feels. There is a tendency in those who feel out of contact with abundance to lose contact with themselves. The two go hand in hand. That is why it is important to stay with yourself throughout this progression of experiences and to trust yourself.

5. Let Go.

Now let it go. Take a deep breath, and notice that you have completed the circuit. The active work has been done. In following steps one through four you have given yourself a great gift. You have strongly cleared, attuned, and aligned with yourself. You need do no more.

You may have your marching boots on, ready to charge forward and pursue the things you want, the abundance you seek. If that is a true desire—motion that still wants to be expressed or enlivened intention for reaching a goal—then follow it. If it is not motion that wants to be expressed, but is instead your thinking or feeling that you must do more or should do more, then give yourself permission to let it go, for it is an illusion. You have done your work and you can sit down now. You can go back about your life and allow yourself to receive.

6. *Receive.*

Allow the effects of your work to come through in your life. Simply allow yourself to receive what you want. Abundance cannot be attained, taken, grabbed, or sought. Neither can the sun and the moon and the stars. You can only step into their light, into their presence, and receive them. Steps one through five have been the steps for moving into the light of abundance, and step six is simply receiving it.

What you want may come to you in the form that you wanted it, or it may not. The important thing is to see it when it comes and to know that the form is not significant. The essence of your desire is what comes back to you fulfilled, not necessarily the form itself. You must be able to see with different eyes so that you may recognize the essence of what you see.

————————————— ◆ —————————————

The feeling of desire comes about because you feel separate from what you want. It is as though a shield of glass stands between you and abundance. You can see the abundance on the other side. You can occasionally see other people going up and taking part in the abundance, then turning around and telling you how to do the same. Yet the glass remains. Your work with these steps can help the glass dissolve. Then you will begin to see that what you wanted was never far away, never separate from you at all.

24

Manifesting

You already have unlimited ability to create in physical reality. The fact is that you are involved in the creation of physical reality all the time. At this very moment, just by being who you are, you are creating the next moment and the next and the next. You could say, for example, that the next six months of your life are created already, not in fate but in possibility, just by your being who you are in this moment.

In your essence, you are an unlimited spirit who has come into physical form. It is through your physical body that your spirit communicates with physical reality, and it is through your physical body that your inner creative force moves outward into the physical world to manifest. Most important to know about this process is that your experience of self is what creates every aspect of your life.

Everything is energy.

Physical matter is energy. Thoughts are energy. Feelings are energy. Every image, thought, feeling, and belief you consciously or unconsciously hold about yourself carries a specific energy formula or pattern to it. These energy patterns are complex and very real. Collectively they make up your "experience of self," which is your inner reality. This ongoing inner reality creates the outer reality you live with every day.

Your auric field is the energy space extending outward from your body. It links your inner experience with the outer world. Through your auric field, the precise energy patterns of your experience of self are transmitted outward into the physical world. There they take form, or manifest, as your life. These energy patterns create all your outer experiences (situations, relationships, prosperity, etc.) and your responses to them. So everything you encounter in life is a reflection of your inner experience of yourself! In that way, your experience of everyone and everything is a mirror for you and is also subject to change as your experience of self changes.

It is said that you reap what you sow.
This is because whatever you emanate,
you will encounter.

If you are aware of yourself as love, for example, those energy patterns are transmitted outward through the auric field, and what you encounter in your life will be the manifested experience of that love. Then the world may seem to you to be a loving place, or at least a more loving place than it would seem if you were not so conscious of your inner source of love.

On a practical level, consider also that the experience of self you carry will determine what actions you take in life. If you carry conscious love of self, you will tend to take actions that are loving and will then reap more loving responses from the world. If you are not in touch with the deep love of your being and do not cherish and honor yourself, your energetic patterning of "nonlove" is sent outward through your auric field into the world and manifested in your life. You may encounter situations over and over in which you are not loved, not honored, not treated as kindly as you would like to be treated. Life can then be a frightening and alienating experience.

As you consider this example of love, understand that you are not bad or flawed for not loving self more, only hungry for the nourishment you deserve. When you are caught in such limitation, it is always possible to open to greater experience. Remember, the change begins within you.

You alter your patterns of outer manifestation by altering your inner experience of self.

Be willing to allow yourself greater love. Nurture that love of self in spite of what life seems to be giving you or telling you. Then you will automatically be adding more self-love to your energy patterning, which transmits outward for manifestation. After a period of time the world will seem to change and you will encounter more love in your life. You will begin to find yourself treated more honorably and cherished more often. You will be more supported in outwardly living the love that is your true nature.

25

Empowering Your Desires

Your manifesting energy never stops working for you. As a highly creative and purposeful force, it literally enables you to interact with projected forms of your being everywhere you go. To whatever degree your experience of self includes inner nurturing and support, your outer relationships will show nurturing and support. To whatever degree you inwardly experience abundance, your outer manifestations will be of abundance. Yet, nothing you manifest in physical reality is important in and of itself. It is all there purely as your reflection for learning and growth. Every person, thing, and situation you encounter is symbolic of some aspect of you.

The sole purpose of manifesting anything is simply to make your experience of self real in physical reality. When you insist on manifesting something for any other purpose, you are at cross-purposes with your own nature. That in itself can be very frustrating and can leave you wondering, "Why isn't what I want coming to me? Why isn't it happening?"

When you have that feeling, let it remind you to drop to a deeper level of awareness. If you find yourself in a situation of being very attached to having more money, a relationship, a new car, a better job, or whatever, and you do not seem to be getting it, experiment with looking at the situation differently. Be aware that your desire for the thing (the money, relationship, car, etc.) is a desire from the most superficial level of your being: your personality.

Although you may be more aware of your personality than you are of the deeper levels of your being, your personality carries the least power. (It is the most oriented to control, but it carries the least true power.) Because the deeper levels of self are progressively more aligned with true self, they carry progressively more manifesting power. You can activate this greater power by simply shifting your awareness. Attuning to the following four levels will take you progressively deeper: (1) Superficial Desire; (2) Essence Desire; (3) Internalized Desire; (4) Desire for True Self.

Each superficial desire
is a symbol
for a greater desire
you hold at a deeper level.

1. Superficial Desire

Your personality is most familiar with superficial desire, which is the desire for things (and situations) that you assume will bring happiness or fulfillment. This desire is reinforced by cultural messages that achievement, material gain, and other people affirm your sense of self and your well-being.

Of the four levels, superficial desires are noticed most frequently. Yet they take the most exertion to pursue and are the least satisfying, even when fulfilled. Recognizing that your superficial desires are incomplete in themselves frees you to look for your deeper power.

*You can empower yourself
by going directly to
the essence of your desire.*

2. Essence Desire

It is easy to let your awareness drop from the superficial to the essence level by asking yourself, "What is the essence of this desire? What is the quality in my life or experience of myself that I want from this?"

For example, money is the most common desire at the superficial level. Yet, money is a symbol for many things. What is the essence level of money for you? Perhaps you feel that when money comes it will bring you a sense of ease in the world. Having your basic financial needs met can indeed bring a certain type of ease. Or maybe having more vacations would bring you joy. Or maybe you simply want the feeling of being supported in life.

The essence of what you want is the feeling or quality that would come into your life by getting the thing (money) that you're focused on. The ease or joy or support is always a deeper desire than the money is. And regardless of how often it may appear otherwise, you always want the essence more than you want the thing.

Let your personality's superficial desires serve as your springboard to the essence level. Each time you catch yourself wanting a "thing," stop and deepen the dialogue. Remind yourself of the truth. "I want more money" becomes "What is it I really want? Oh yes, now I feel it. The essence of what I really want is more peace (or ease, or joy, etc.) in my life." Or it may be "I want to feel supported in the world. I want to feel supported in being who I am and in having what I need." When you're willing to make this shift, wanting a thing (money, a relationship, or whatever) automatically reminds you of your deeper desire.

Let the essence level of desire be real to you. Allow it to become a part of your awareness every day so you can stay in touch with what you actually want. When the essence of your desire becomes real to you daily, it stimulates a shift in your pattern of manifesting. As the essence awareness integrates into your life, it becomes part of your experience of self and energetically supports the direct creation of what you truly want.

You can still want more money, a relationship, a car, or a new job. There is nothing wrong with wanting on the superficial level; that's part of living in the physical world, too. But if you assume that getting the thing will somehow make up for what you're missing at the essence level, you put yourself on a treadmill of dissatisfaction. Staying focused exclusively on the thing can enable you to get it, yet nothing will have changed at the essence level because that was not where you put your focus. You will have gotten the symbol but not the essence that the symbol represents. You will have the money you wanted, but still not have enough true ease or joy or support in your life. If even then you do not change your focus to the essence level of wanting, you may soon find yourself chasing another symbol, another thing, in the hope that it will save you.

If you wonder why you never quite get what you want, look closely at that dynamic because it is basic to manifesting. Remember that you always really want the essence more than the thing. As you allow your essence desire to be as real, or more real, to you than your desire for the thing, you are well on your way to manifesting it.

Essence desire is wanting
meaningful qualities in your life;
internalized desire is wanting
them in yourself.

3. *Internalized Desire*

This desire brings your focus even closer to Home. For example, perhaps your essence desire says, "I want to feel supported in the world." It can then prompt you to drop to the level in which you want to feel more supported by you. "I want to feel more support for myself from myself." This support is not based on your achieving any particular outer standard of being worthy or deserving. It is a basic need for unconditional support of self—a support of self that does not fluctuate according to outer realities such as your financial situation or other people's feelings about you. Or, if you want more joy in your life, look within for the level of self in which you want inner joy that is not taken away by changes in outer events or relationships.

Beneath the desire for all things
and all qualities of experience,
inner and outer,
lies the desire
to discover your true nature.

4. *Desire for True Self*

Desire for true self says something like this: "More than any-thing, I want to manifest who I fully am so that I may see and recognize my true self as real." The desire for true self is so basic that every spirit who comes into physical form has it. It is especially strong during infancy and childhood, the very times when there seems to be the least recognition and support for it from other people. Fulfillment of this desire involves bridging the split between inner potential and outer reality. It means sensing your true self within and manifesting it outwardly in the world, where it becomes real to you.

Imagine reclaiming your true self and living it daily. Imag-ine bringing your unlimited spirit through into physical form *and recognizing it.* That is liberation. That is freedom. That is coming Home.

Living from true self brings you to such an inner state of unity (you are united with all aspects of your being) that it also opens you to unity with all things and all beings: human, ani-mal, earth, and spirit. When you are in this state, you already have everything you want. And when you recognize your true self manifested in the world, manifesting things like money, a car, relationships, or a job becomes child's play. So don't be sur-prised if, in your return to true self, you lose interest in creating some things that had been important to you before. When you have learned to drop beneath the symbols to create what you've always wanted most, the more superficial desires will seem less urgent and more elective.

You may have a tendency to go for the symbols when you don't feel able to go for true self. You may not know what your true self is, your true self may seem impossibly out of reach, or maybe you simply are not aware that a true self even exists. So when you can't get in touch with the deeper possibilities, you automatically gravitate to the more superficial ones. You may even become good at manifesting on the superficial level and creating lots of things in your life. Yet, you are stuck there until you choose to open to greater depths, to *your* greater depths, and plunge in.

◆   ◆   ◆

You may find that most of your time and energy in working with manifesting the fulfillment of your desires goes into levels one, two, and three (and probably in that order). Yet, it is important also to be aware of level four. Working (or playing!) with the deepening levels of desire is a way to move more intimately into yourself and to explore who you are, yet still stay connected with the outer world. You can move back and forth between inner and outer, superficial and deep, and never be in the wrong place.

There is no wrong place in this exploration. All of it is you, and all of it is valuable. Just keep paying attention. The more awareness you bring to this process, the more quickly you will learn.

26

Relinquishing Control

Your essence is light and love. Furthermore, all physical reality is only the manifestation of light and the manifestation of love in innumerable forms.

Let's look at what this means. When you feel the emotion of love, it is easy to identify that as a manifestation of love. Likewise, when you sense a radiance or lightness to your spirit, that is easily a manifestation of light. Yet these obvious examples are only the tip of the iceberg. All experiences convey light and love, from the most mundane to the most unusual, and many go unrecognized for the profound potential they carry.

Any situation in your life that is difficult is as much a manifestation of love as is a pleasant one. For example, think of an experience you've had that seemed to bring pain or discomfort into your life. You may remember how distressing it felt and how much you resisted it. You may still think of it as a negative experience. Clearly, that situation didn't look or feel as if it was a manifestation of light or love, yet it was. It came to you full of possibilities for learning—graced for growth. When you genuinely recognize all occurrences as vehicles for light and love, a quality of richness and surrender enters your life. There is a deep connection, a sense of peace, openness, and safety that you cannot find without accepting this basic truth.

When you see and know and feel
the reality of light and love in all
of life's experiences, you are released
from the grip of belief in nonabundance.

This idea may prompt you to think, "Okay, whatever is going on in my life is light and love. Some of it feels good, some of it feels bad, but it is all light and love. So how do I control these manifestations of light and love to create more good experiences and fewer bad ones?"

When you have experiences that feel comfortable or exciting or wonderful, there is a tendency to think, "Right now things are going just as they should. Things are good." Such a belief implies that when things are not comfortable and do not feel so good, it means that something is wrong, that things are not going well, that it is a bad situation. When you think of experiences as being good or bad, positive or negative, you limit yourself and close yourself off from important avenues of growth.

From the perspective of unlimited spirit, when things are uncomfortable—perhaps you are in pain, uncertainty, or fear—nothing is necessarily wrong. It is simply that you are embracing life as a human being in the midst of discomfort. Love and light are still present in that experience, no matter what the situation is or how uncomfortable it may be.

You cannot control your manifesting to the point that you create only experiences you think are positive, meaning that they feel good to you. To some degree you must allow life to present itself to you without control. It is quite all right to say to yourself, "I want to manifest work that reflects who I really am and gives me the opportunity to express my true self in the world." It's also fine to say, "I want to create more financial support and a greater sense of ease in my life," or "I want to have loving relationships; I want to experience an openness in my heart that I have not yet felt in this lifetime." But it is limiting to add, " . . . and I am not open to anything else."

That type of control makes you resist some of your most potentially expansive experiences if there is pain or loss involved. A situation that causes grief, for example, is often thought of as a bad thing to manifest because it is so uncomfortable. In fact, your mind may say that you would be crazy to wish for something that brings you grief. And yet, in its deeper wisdom, your true self knows that grief can cleanse the system and open the heart in a powerful way. So you may actually will an experience of grief to yourself because of all it has to offer.

Understand that you do not usually will grief (or pain, illness, suffering, and so on) to yourself at the conscious, personality level. In fact, your personality will often emphatically resist such experiences and deny any part in their manifestation. But remember that your personality is the most superficial aspect of your being (the most "removed" from true self) and, therefore, has the least true power. Your true self has much greater power in manifesting. It uses this power to create precisely the situations that offer you the most perfect growth. At that level of deep compassion and expanded insight, you will all your experiences to yourself.

*Every thought,
conscious or unconscious,
is powerful.*

Your thoughts literally create your reality—past, present, and future. By consciously directing your thoughts, you can use their power to align with the deep level of self that guides your life. This alignment can be particularly effective in transforming your experience of distress. For example, when you are facing a personal difficulty, you can stop for a moment, take a deep breath, and—without denying any of your distress—choose for that situation to be a vehicle for deep empowerment. Take a moment to affirm something like, "I open to all that I am. I align with higher truth, with higher light, with higher love. Through this situation, I allow the energy of my true self to move into my life."

Sometimes you will feel the effects of this affirmation immediately. Other times you may not feel anything right away. Trust the thought of alignment anyway, and pause for a deep shift to take place, even though it may be so subtle that you cannot feel it consciously. Your intention is powerful, and the shift will take place regardless of whether you feel it. Subtle shifts happen at a core energy level and lay the groundwork for future experiences that will noticeably match your affirmation.

If you do this process of alignment and have even the most subtle sensation that something has shifted—perhaps your spine stands just a bit taller, your facial muscles have relaxed a little, or you have a new feeling of lightness—notice it. However subtle, however insignificant it may seem, acknowledge it. "I accept the light, and I allow the subtlety of it."

When you understand the power of such subtle experience, you take a lot less for granted in life. By attuning to the very subtle shifts that occur in response to your directed thought and feeling, you begin to truly understand and witness how you affect your reality in each moment.

Reality is created
tiny bit by tiny bit.

Imagine that your current life, your current reality, is a great puzzle made up of microscopic pieces that you put together. Some areas are still in the process of being assembled, so the puzzle is incomplete. Each time you align with a subtle shift within yourself, you take a new piece to that puzzle and press it into place. This is a self-directed way of literally putting your life together as you go along. By consciously choosing what you attune to, you are creating the content of the puzzle and the forms of your life.

27

Owning Your Power to Create

As you think about consciously creating your life, you may wish you were better at manifesting. Yet, the truth is that you are already manifesting most excellently in every moment! Just look at your life and see how much has come to you. Whether it's happiness, sadness, fear, doubt, pain, joy, or lightness of spirit, your life is a rich blend of what it is to be alive and vital and full of human experiences.

Your very ability to create in physical reality is what has enabled you to be here in the first place. A being who does not have the inherent ability to manifest would never get into physical reality. To be here you must first manifest yourself into physical form. After you have done that, you naturally have the ability to manifest anything in your life, and you never lose that ability.

*You are the creator of your life;
at some level you have wanted
or needed every experience
you have encountered.*

Recognition of this truth is a fundamental step toward more conscious manifesting. It allows you to recognize the power you have been using all along and to begin to direct it with intention. Yet, you may find that you have some resistance to this idea. Believing that you have created your life and have wanted all that you've created can be frightening to your personality. Your personality often forgets that greater levels of your being are in charge.

If you are unhappy with your work and you don't have enough money to pay the bills, your personality may refuse to accept that you created such an "undesirable" situation. It may say, "I'd be stupid to create this!" It may think that taking responsibility for creating your life means having to blame yourself, as though creating such a challenging or uncomfortable situation is a negative thing.

Your personality forgets that the deeper soul of your being views your life from a different vantage point. Perhaps your personality doesn't want the situation of having a job you hate and insufficient money to cover your bills; but perhaps your soul does choose that situation. Your soul may see that through that challenge you will learn important lessons: lessons about who you truly are, what your spiritual relationship with money is, or how clearing your issues with money can heal a deeper inner struggle.

The soul's teachings are usually
much broader than anything
the personality
can grasp right away.

You may not be able to completely understand what your lesson is about until you have lived it through. That's how your soul teaches your personality—by living. So, until you have lived through the deeper teaching enough to really understand it, let yourself be unknowing! Also, let yourself surrender to the sense that, somewhere deep within, you have wanted and created each situation in your life and that you love yourself enough to open to the learning it brings.

If you think that owning your power to manifest means that you must blame yourself for your "misfortunes," see if you can open your heart to a new compassion that will gently melt the self-blame. Your manifestations are never wrong or bad. They may sometimes be uncomfortable, painful, or over-whelming, but they are always for a deeper purpose. Always.

Maybe you are used to blaming others (other people or outside circumstances) for some of your difficulties or pain. This is a very human thing to do, and almost everyone has this tendency. Owning your power to manifest disrupts this pattern of blaming others, and your personality may respond with resistance to this change.

Three major forms of resistance may surface.

1. ***Fear of Shifting the Blame.***　If your personality needs to blame other people or situations ("He is the cause of my unhappiness." "You can't buck the system." "That's just how life is."), it will be afraid to let go of outer blame, as though its defenses are being taken away. Here the basic premise is, "It must be *somebody's* fault; if it's not their fault then it must be mine." Within that belief, if you take

the blame off others it automatically falls back onto you. That feels uncomfortable, unfair, and debilitating; no wonder you resist it!

2. *Fear of Losing Your Power.* Your personality may assume that taking responsibility for creating your life means automatically letting everyone else off the hook for his or her behavior. If you hold yourself accountable, but feel you no longer can hold other people accountable for themselves, it feels as though they have power and you don't. You feel weakened and forced into a passive role. No wonder you resist this, too!

3. *Fear of Being Stuck.* You may have a hidden belief that if you avoid responsibility for something uncomfortable in your life, it will go away—or at least be less real. The flip side is the fear that if you do claim what you have created and face it straight on, its reality will be reinforced and locked in even more. The assumption is that you will then be stuck repeating the pattern, caught in it for good. Here again, you resist.

Ironically, in spite of these beliefs, to the degree that you distance yourself from whatever you have manifested in your life, you are likely to continue to manifest it. When you consciously or unconsciously say to yourself, "I do not want to look at my power to manifest; I do not want to acknowledge that I've created the difficulty in my life," you are likely to continue to create that very difficulty. You unconsciously create experiences over and over until you own your creation.

By rejecting the idea that you create what you have, you distance yourself from your power and weaken your ability to draw to you what you want. Or, if you reject your current life and try to escape from it into something new, you will find that you never quite seem to get away. It is by fully embracing your current life and loving yourself in the midst of it that you heal what needs to be healed, that you free yourself and are empowered to create and attract something new.

*Living is the act
of surrendering to
and exploring
the life you already have,
learning to love yourself
in the midst of all your creations.*

If you completely accept that you have created your life, you embrace your creative power. Changing your life then becomes much simpler. You can look at a difficult experience and sincerely say, "It feels as if this happened to me, and if feels as if I would be crazy to want this in my life. Yet I see from the heart of my being that I manifested this. I accept that I created this experience out of deep wisdom and love for myself. I open to the learning it has to offer."

If you continue to be unconscious of manifesting everything in your life, you continue to feel that things happen to you. But as you allow yourself to acknowledge and align with your deep creative power, you free yourself to manifest more consciously and compassionately.

Another way of saying this is that when you surrender to the creator within, you surrender to having created everything in your life. You love yourself, instead of judge yourself, in the midst of your creation, no matter how comfortable or uncomfortable your life may be. This surrender is an act of power. People who can do it need to be told very little about how to manifest.

Surrender is not just mental or emotional. It is much deeper. It is the feeling of complete immersion in the experience of yourself as creator of your life and immersion in love of yourself in the midst of your creation. This love does not necessarily mean that you love *what* you've created in your life or even that you particularly have to be comfortable with it, but that you love *yourself* in the midst of it all. From there you will intuitively know how to create what you want for yourself in the future. In fact, as you sit in that immersion, whatever you think and deeply feel you want in your life is instantly put into the programming for future manifestation. When you have the experience of yourself as manifestor, you are able to consciously direct that manifesting ability to enrich any area of your life you choose.

28

Transforming Your Blocks

Major transitions are not always easy. It takes time to live new truths. Sometimes as you go through transformation, it seems as though every personal pattern that ever held you back becomes stronger or comes at you from a new angle. You may find yourself caught in feelings or memories of being unloved and alone. Emotional pain and despair may surface. Rigid beliefs of "can't have" and "don't deserve" may seem to get the better of you for a while. You can become confused or frustrated or doubtful that you are making progress.

Remember that it's all right if this happens. It does not mean that you are losing ground or that you will not be successful in your growth. It simply means that you have been willing to drop into yourself at a deeper level. This commitment to new depth is like a light that shines into the dark corners of your unconscious, flushing out everything at that level that is still holding you back and keeping you separate from true self. These shadows are unclaimed aspects of your being, areas or issues where you have been afraid to "turn on the light" before. Now, out of love of self, you are allowing these issues to come forward to be faced and embraced.

> *Each area of darkness*
> *is your offering to the light*
> *of your true being.*

Each transition through the darkness is a sacred rite of passage, performed out of great love for self and willingness to become whole no matter what the challenge. You are moving into greater abundance; open your heart to yourself and proceed, allowing each shadow to make its way to the light as it is drawn out for healing.

In the midst of this transition, your inner blocks to fulfilling your true desires can seem very real. In dealing with this issue, understand that no block is a real block; that is, no block has power of its own. A block appears real because you experience it and because it seems to affect you. But the moment you come to a true inner readiness and willingness to move through your old pattern, the block loses its power.

Simply allow yourself to add something greater to your limited beliefs. You rarely have to get rid of a limited experience or belief to grow beyond it. What is most empowering is simply adding something to it that will help you expand.

> *The truth will always*
> *help you expand.*

Your blocks are the areas where your personality identifies with limitation. Sometimes you may feel as though your personality has the most control over you, but because it is the most superficial aspect of your being, it always has the least true power. As we have seen, the greatest power comes from the deepest core of your being: your true, unlimited self. As you move inward, or deeper, from your personality, each level of awareness carries greater truth and, therefore, greater power. In other words, the more closely aligned with true self your awareness is, the more power it carries.

For example, the belief of "can't have" can remain, undisturbed, and you can still have what you want. If you allow yourself to hold two levels of awareness around a given issue, the deeper awareness will always carry more power and, over time, will transform the more superficial belief. So if you hold your personality's belief in limitation ("I can't have") alongside the deeper truth of essence desire ("I want greater ease") or essence abundance ("I am willing to have"), the deeper truth will prevail.

It may take time and repetition—remembering to attune to the deeper level whenever a block seems to be stopping you—but sooner or later the deeper truth will transform your block. That is why you do not have to reject or fight your block. When it becomes your habit to open to the deeper level, your block will be transformed naturally by the greater power of the deeper truth. This process can also give tremendous support to other approaches you may be exploring for mental, emotional, or energetic clearing.

Truth
always transforms
nontruth.

The truth of your being is a brilliant light that will shine into the shadows of your less true self, transforming the dark to light whenever you offer those shadows to it. You make your offering with your awareness. When you recognize a limiting belief or desire, let your awareness move to a deeper level, to the greater belief that already exists along with the limited one or to the deeper desire below the superficial one.

As the greater truth transforms the lesser one, the energy that went into maintaining your limitation begins to go into expanding your experience. Similarly, all the old energy that seemed to work against you or block your way now serves you by clearing your path and propelling you forward into greater growth.

So, alongside the belief of "I cannot have and I do not deserve; everyone gets to have what they want but me," add something greater. Remember what you truly are: love. From that love, remember what you truly want. Then allow yourself that true wanting even though your conditioning or habit of thought tells you that you cannot have it. "I want the feeling of support in my life. I'm willing to receive it even though I feel that I do not deserve it." "I want joy or ease in my life even though I've always felt it was meant for others rather than for me. I want it anyway, and I'm willing to have it." This is most empowering. None of your limitations is ever truly stopping you. The universe is very generous, and you can always have what you truly want or need. You just need to be willing.

As you move into this shift of awareness, the mental conditioning that had been holding you back may still continue speaking to you, saying things like, "You are not good enough." "You do not deserve to get what you want." "You cannot have it. If you get it you will just lose it again." Perhaps you also still have people around you who reflect that limited belief by remaining unsupportive of you. But now, even in the midst of that old limitation, you have greater choice. Without resisting the limitation, you can add a greater reality to it, one that empowers you. You can allow yourself to have.

When that old, unsupportive voice comes forward, you do not need to push it away. Simply acknowledge it. Say, "Here it is again." Then acknowledge and choose the new reality: "In spite of everything, I want what I want, and I'm willing to have it!" Align with the new voice, claim the deeper truth, and feel it in your body.

When you align this way daily, that new voice becomes as real to you as the old one—and, in time, even more real. Your attunement to truth deepens, and your overall experience of self grows to include having what you truly want. As this takes place, your outer life begins to shift and reflect the change.

Keep in mind that things do not change for you because you are a good person, because you are spiritual enough, or because you dress well. These are all equally arbitrary assessments and do not matter. It is what you hold in your experience of self that determines what you create in your life. When you can allow yourself to remember your essence, feel your true desires, and receive fulfillment, so much more can come to you.

◆

Attunement
Being Creator of Your Life #1

As you go about your life, stop for a moment several times a day to look at your life. Regardless of what you are doing, thinking, or feeling in the moment, say to yourself, "Yes, I have created this, and I love myself in this creation." Truly sink into the feeling of being the creator of your life. Doing this perhaps ten to twelve times a day for a week will help bring a shift in your awareness and in your ability to be truly with yourself in your life.

When you say, "I love myself," sometimes you will feel it and sometimes you won't; either way is all right. Sometimes self-love is noticeable alongside other feelings. Other times, intense emotion may completely overshadow the feeling of love of self, which tends to be of a more subtle vibration.

If you do not feel the love, breathe. Look within as though you are looking for the most subtle colors of a sunset. If you find a subtle feeling of love of self, then breathe to acknowledge and receive it. If you still do not feel the love at all, do not worry. It does not mean that it is not there or that you are doing the exercise incorrectly. Your act of inner alignment has power whether or not you are able to feel it at the most conscious level. It will be working at a deeper level and will surface in time.

◆

Attunement
Being Creator of Your Life #2

For a week, take some time each day to scan your life. Allow yourself to recognize that you have already manifested a wealth of human experiences. Whether the feelings are pleasant or unpleasant does not matter. During the few minutes of scanning your life, you are being with yourself as you are now and are noticing how much you have already created.

During this week, also consider allowing yourself to let go temporarily of the desire to change anything about your life that is not absolutely necessary. It can be liberating to take a week's vacation from feeling that anything is wrong and that you must do something about it.

This exercise may bring up the fear that you will be condoning everything in your life and will, therefore, be stuck with it as it is. Your mind may want to focus on change to avoid things as they are. But in spite of that reaction, see if you can allow yourself to take a vacation from trying, or even wanting, to change anything.

You may choose to balance the desire for change with a thought or affirmation such as the following: "I allow myself to receive learning and empowerment from everything I have already created in my life" or "I surrender to all I have created at this time, and I trust that it will guide me in growth." As always with affirmations, use wording that is simple and feels right for you.

The first lesson in being able to direct your manifesting powers more consciously is to allow what you have already done to be enough. As you stop running away from what you are living with right now, you begin to allow yourself to embrace your life as it is. You cannot accept yourself if you feel you must run away from what you have already created by quickly creating something better. Open your heart to the present and learn from all that you have manifested. You are complete in this moment. You are an excellent manifestor already.

------------------ ◆ ------------------

Attunement
Being Creator of Your Life #3

Each night as you lie down to sleep, compassionately align with yourself as manifestor of your life. Feel your body relax as you think and feel the following: "I open to true wisdom and compassion in the heart of my being. I align with myself as manifestor and creator of my life. I allow this knowledge to become real to me." Adjust the wording to whatever feels most appropriate to you.

------------------ ◆ ------------------

---◆---

Meditation

Being Creator of Your Life #4

1. Sit quietly for a few moments and feel the gentle movement of your breath. . . . Allow your attention to drop into your heart. Feel your heart's openness and warmth. . . .

2. From within your heart, think or feel the following: "I align within the heart of my being, home of deep wisdom and compassion. . . . I call forward this wisdom and compassion to help me fully experience the life I have already created. . . . From my heart I align with myself as manifestor. . . . I am vibrant and I am aligned, always. . . ."

3. Sit for a few minutes longer in the reverberations of your affirmation. When you are ready to come out of meditation, breathe fully and become aware of the rest of your body. Then slowly open your eyes, stretch and move, and get up when you are ready.

---◆---

Part VI
Enlivened Emotion

◆

The Healing Power
of Intense Feeling

29

Emotion as a Vehicle for Spirit

Emotion is the current of life moving through the physical body. Through emotion, refined spirit can become real to us at the denser levels of our being. To the degree that we either open to or resist emotion, we open to or resist unlimitedness as it circulates within the density of our human selves.

Notice how you respond to the thought of having a dense level to your being. You may not be pleased to consider yourself dense, and your first reaction may be to deny your density or to want to transform your density as soon as possible. Perhaps you think, "Density can't be good. I want to be spiritual and refined. I don't want to be dense."

Rejoice in your density! The glory of life in physical form is about coming into density and delighting in it. When you were an infant, you delighted in everything about the physical world, including its density. To eyes that still recognized essence everywhere, the density of emotion gave off brilliant color and in some ways was far more fascinating than the refinement of spirit.

So reconsider the density of emotion. Love the density of your human self. Claim it. In fact, insist on having your share of density! It is what you came here for, and you have a right to explore it.

Whatever you resist becomes a burden.

Some people resist the unlimitedness of refined spirit and interpret the spiritual aspect of life to be a burden; it becomes a heavy cross to bear. On the other hand, if emotion is resisted there is a loss of the joy of density, seemingly making the denser aspects of life a struggle or oppressive. Yet, as emotion is accepted and explored, felt and integrated, it creates a stronger

connection with self as well as a deeper awareness of the interconnectedness of all people and all things.

Emotions are fluid. They have no set boundaries that keep
them separate from each other. Any deeply felt emotion has the
potential of opening the way for other emotions. For example,
perhaps you have been so busy working on a project for several
months that you haven't had a chance to be aware of your feelings. Then the project is completed and you have time off. As
your pace slows, you begin to feel emotions you did not realize
were there.

Perhaps sadness is one of them. As you stay with your feelings, the sadness becomes a deep grief. You join a support
group so you can have a safe place to feel and talk about your
grieving. At some point as you move through the grief, you
notice that a new joy begins to come into your life. You become
aware that feeling your grief has cleared the space for the
deeper joy to be felt also. The fluidity of emotion and your
willingness to ride its current have guided you into a more
vibrant intimacy with yourself.

It is also possible that the grief (or any other deeply felt
emotion) may spontaneously make you aware of your connection to all other people who feel or have felt that emotion.
Emotion is an energy that does not belong to anyone, does not
begin or end within the person who feels it. Each emotion
flows through all physical beings, connecting them at the
deepest level of physical awareness.

So, the grief you feel is not your grief; it is *the* grief that
flows through all people. Similarly, the sadness or joy or love
you feel is not yours, but is a universal energy you are tapping
into and interpreting in your own terms. As you open to this
emotion in your life, it becomes a vibrant expression of your
connection with self and others.

If you have a long-standing pattern of resisting emotion,
you probably adopted that pattern in response to early envi-

ronmental pressure. Perhaps your family upbringing, reinforced by experiences in society, taught you to resist or deny
your feelings. If your current environment continues to reinforce your loss of emotional vitality rather than support you in
reclaiming it, you may very well feel unable to change. Opening to deeply resisted emotion can feel too threatening without
compassionate, reliable outside support.

You do not have to open to emotion alone. In fact, you may
not be able to do it alone. If it was a restrictive environment
that caused you to close off to such an important aspect of your
being, it may take an equally supportive environment to enable
you to open again. You deserve to reclaim your vibrant emotional self and, with it, the joy of density. You have every right
to an environment of true support.

Finding that environment is the challenge. Seeking emotional support and not giving up if you have trouble finding it
is in itself important work. Sometimes people say, "I cannot
find the right friends, the right therapist, the right group, the
right technique," and so on. Maybe that has been true for you,
too, up to this point, but how strong is your insistence? How
committed are you? How demanding of life are you willing to
be to create your supportive environment?

It may not always be easy to find what you are seeking, but
that does not mean it is not available. Whatever you truly long
for is always available. That is a given in life. How you get yourself to it is a mirror of your commitment to self, your commitment to reclaiming the brilliance of being fully alive.

Your container for spirit
in this lifetime is your dense self.

Your personality includes your thoughts, emotions, and
physical body as well as your relationship with the outer world
and other people. It is the container you use to carry unlimited

spirit as you move through the world. To the degree that you resist the density of that container, you restrict your ability to carry conscious awareness of spirit. If you have aspirations to be highly spiritual, take loving care of your human self, for that is truly the divine work.

30

Love

As you came into this lifetime, you brought memory of the truth of your being. Unlimitedness of spirit was still real to you, and you carried a capacity for love so complete that there was no separation. You were indeed one with all things and all beings.

As we have already seen, you then became acculturated to the environment in which you grew up (your family, your social environment, and society in general) and took on the beliefs and experiences that surrounded you. This cultural conscious-ness was not based on unlimited being; it told you that, in fact, you were not one with others. Much of infancy and early child-hood was spent learning that here in physical reality you are viewed and responded to as though you are completely sepa-rate. In return, you were required to display that reality of separation through your actions, your communication, and your inner experience. Through that separation, your sense of self and your sense of reality became more limited.

That phase in your personality development was an im-portant part of your adaptation to physical reality and its lim-ited consciousness. You came here to be in the physical world, and you took on the conditioning of physical consciousness to explore this reality more deeply.

Now, from the midst of your exploration of the separation and limitation of physical reality, you are starting to reopen to greater memory once more. This time you are inviting the awareness of true self slowly to become integrated into your personality, into the aspect of your being that has embodied the limited consciousness prevalent in the physical realm. At the core of this integration is the discovery that you no longer have to be restricted to choosing between submersion into the apparent limitation of physical reality or expansion into the freedom of unlimited being. It does not have to be either/or anymore. From the midst of any limited experience, you can open to unlimited self.

*You are developing the skill to contain
and carry both the limited
and the unlimited together.*

The integration of unlimited being into a reality previously based on limitation will ultimately be successful throughout the planetary culture. This success has already been destined, not by some powerful "outside" force or being, but by the collective consciousness of all beings involved. All beings bringing that destiny into reality, including you, have chosen their parts with care.

As you reclaim your deep memory of true self and unity with all things and all beings, you remember that this unity is based on unconditional love. Beings who are aligned in true self tap into a deep level from which they are flooded with unlimited love and the feeling of true Home. This deep love naturally radiates outward and connects them energetically and spiritually with all other beings, physical and nonphysical.

All people desire this state of truth and love, whether or not they are conscious of it. Every person who has a deep feeling of longing to go Home is longing for that state where nothing can interfere with the deep connection between self and others. What is so painful in the world is that there seem to be too many experiences that keep people from feeling their true connection with themselves and each other.

31

Hate

This is where hate comes in. At a basic level, hate is an outlet for the outrage at being separated from the deeply loving aspect of true self. Because of its intensity and extreme discomfort, hate then also becomes another of those separating experiences, adding further to a vicious cycle. As hate blocks your deep, loving connection with self and others, the world seems more dangerous. More energy goes into defending and protecting yourself, which reinforces separation and takes you further away from conscious connection with true self.

For a moment, remember a situation when you hated another person. Your feeling in that situation may have been extreme rage and hatred, or it may have simply been hate in the form of anger that you could not seem to get over, the sort of anger that ate at you day after day. Perhaps your hate was due to something specific that person said or did.

No matter what the hate seemed to be about, looking deeper into it would probably reveal that the event that inspired your hate brought up feelings that separated you from your connection with true self. You lost contact with your true state of love of self because of that other person's actions, thoughts, or feelings. And because you lost connection with your true self, you then lost the ability to feel a deep level of unconditional love and connection to other people, particularly to the person you hated.

Remember, your most basic, true state is to be in unlimited love and connection with all beings. This unity brings a sense of inner peace and safety that is your greatest treasure. When someone does something that stimulates a response within you that blocks your ability to feel loving connection, it's as though you are cut off from your greatest well-being in a brutal way. Then not only do you feel hurt by what the person did, but also you suffer the injury of losing your connection to true self.

> *Losing your natural ability to love both*
> *yourself and the person who hurt you*
> *is the greatest loss possible.*

It is very threatening when someone else's actions can take away your connection to true self and, therefore, your basic sense of well-being and safety in the world. All hate is anguish at the loss of self and the ability to feel loved and loving. There is terror and outrage that someone else has the power to cut you off from that love. If your true state of being can be taken away by what other people say and do, indeed, the world will seem brutal and unsafe.

Often the response to this threat is to defend yourself by positioning for battle—mentally, emotionally, physically. As you know, the cultural conditioning of physical reality tells you that when you are threatened, you make war. There are more wars happening in the world at this time than you can keep track of, and some are taking place within your own life.

Being at war does not necessarily mean that you attack in an outer way. You may simply carry on a long inner experience of war, hating people for what they have done to you or have taken from you. This may manifest as a list of things you believe to be wrong with them, things they shouldn't have done, ways they caused you or others pain, defects in their character, and so on.

Your list may be very accurate and may even reflect issues that truly need to be worked out. Yet your most basic concern really is, "What do I do about releasing myself from this stance of war so I can reconnect with my true self? How can I reopen to the unlimited love that connects me with all life?"

Bringing greater inner connection back into your life takes frequent renewal of your intention. It means choosing to add a more expanded awareness to whatever feelings you are having in the moment. Remember that you never have to stop your feelings, even if they seem limiting to you. You simply need to be creative about letting yourself extend beyond the limitations of those feelings.

Hatred can be a very limiting emotion, giving you the sense of being closed off as though there is nothing that exists but that uncomfortable feeling. Your heart feels closed, and you are frustrated at not being able to loosen the grip your hatred has on you.

When you feel stuck in the emotion of hating, you can use the discomfort to remind yourself of your desire to bring greater light into that aspect of your personality. You can pause for a moment and affirm, "Even in the midst of this feeling, I choose to remember my connection to true self and unlimited being."

Sometimes the hate will be so powerful that there does not seem to be room for any other feeling. You may still need to deal with your anger and hate constructively, in practical terms, yet your affirmation will be laying the energetic circuitry to hold a more expanded experience in the future.

Even one second of affirmation has a powerful effect, regardless of whether you feel it in the moment. The greatest effect takes place at a level deeper than feeling. So if you repeat your affirmation sincerely even a hundred times over a period of days or weeks without feeling the connection, there will still be an accumulative effect of all those seconds. At some point your inner circuitry will become strong enough so that you will begin to notice a difference.

Sooner or later you will notice that even in the midst of hating there can still be a connection with true self and unconditional love. You will begin to stay open to love even when you feel hate. Then hate will no longer limit you; it will no longer separate you from love and expanded awareness. Hate will no longer be a dangerous, destructive feeling that must be avoided or denied; it will be just another human feeling through which the light of truth can shine and bring transformation.

What a glorious breakthrough! At that point you will genuinely be able to hold more than one reality in your consciousness at a time. Do not undervalue this ability; it is the secret to expanding the consciousness and opening to new possibilities. For this reason, it is a recurring theme throughout this book.

Even if you are feeling angry or sad or frustrated or hateful, you can also (simultaneously!) feel your connection with unlimited spirit. It's as though a ray of light shines into the darkness. As you continue to affirm your connection with unlimited being, the ray of light grows. Yet even if the darkness of hate closes your heart and seems bigger than that single ray of light, the ray of light has greater power because it comes from true self.

When you are able to contain both the light and dark together, that is a very enlightening state. It means that you no longer have to choose one experience over another. You do not have to choose love *or* hate, blame *or* forgiveness, sadness *or* joy, anger *or* openheartedness. You are no longer polarized; no particular feeling boxes you in and keeps you from the light of true self. You then have access to the full range of human experiences you came into this life to embrace.

32

Forgiveness

Forgiveness is the antidote for hate: it is the path back to true self. The best suggestion for finding forgiveness in your heart for someone you hate is to find forgiveness for yourself first. Frequently people do not want to focus on forgiving themselves because they think it means they have to admit guilt for something. They think that forgiveness is given only to someone who has done something wrong. It is important to realize that people often need forgiveness even when they have done nothing wrong.

Rather than seeing forgiveness as excusing someone for wrong-doing, see it as simply extending compassion where compassion is needed. Then it becomes easier to forgive everyone, yourself included.

Even if you believe that someone else has wronged or hurt you, forgiving that person (or coming to peace with the situation) may be easier if you extend a hand of true compassion to yourself first. "I forgive myself. In the face of everything this person has done or has put me through, I extend loving compassion to myself. I forgive myself for the pain and anger I have felt."

Remember, there is nothing wrong with your pain and anger, yet forgiving yourself for feeling it may still be important. Intense pain or anger is often accompanied by an automatic sense of guilt, so it can help to realize that beneath your pain, anger, or hatred you may have hidden guilt or shame about those feelings. Because that guilt or shame adds more discomfort, you may unconsciously avoid the whole set of feelings by becoming self-righteous: "Well, they wronged me, so they deserve to have something bad happen to them." "He should come and apologize to me first." "I would never do the kind of thing she did!"

*Whenever you are at war
with someone else, you are always
at war with yourself, too.*

The deep guilt about your feelings is your war against yourself. When you are self-righteous with someone else to avoid feeling your own guilt or shame, you are fighting yourself as much as you are fighting the other person. You have probably already discovered that such a dual battle becomes all-consuming and self-destructive—a war you can never win.

In the midst of this complex web of intense and difficult emotion, how do you create healing so that you can move on? Simply forgiving yourself cuts through everything and returns you to a state of empowerment and simplicity. "I forgive myself for feeling hurt. I forgive myself for anger and hatred. I forgive myself for separating from the true heart of my being."

Or, because forgiving is to give forth compassion, you may feel more comfortable with different wording: "I give myself compassion in the midst of this pain. I give myself compassion in the midst of my anger or hatred. I give myself compassion for having been separated so easily from the truth of my being by what someone else did or said."

Truly giving yourself compassion—not self-righteousness for how you have been wronged or self-pity for how terrible the ordeal has been, but genuine, glowing compassion—softens everything. With that softening, your battle armor begins to melt; your war stance becomes less rigid because you are gaining a truer power. As you continue feeling compassion for yourself in the midst of your human difficulties, the war stance will soften even more. It will happen gently and naturally as you are ready to move into your greater strength.

So it is a matter of extending, from the midst of that position of war, a hand of compassion to self. "Yes, I see the pain, and I give compassion to myself in the midst of it. I remember that even though it may feel impossible at this moment, I want to be reconnected to my unlimited love of self. I want to reclaim the love that streams through my being and unites me with all other beings in peace and truth."

Keep in mind that all current experiences of hate carry a hidden registry of previous, formative experiences when you felt forced into similarly devastating separation from self. You never experience hate that is truly only of the moment. All hate carries the memory and burden of unresolved outrage at having lost your connection to true self in the past. So, a current conflict that brings you to unbearable rage or hatred may be an excellent opportunity to begin deeper healing of your past.

When you find yourself automatically in a war stance from which you feel unable to release either yourself or the person you hate, pay close attention. You may notice that your feelings of hate seem to go beyond the current situation, trailing into your past so deeply that you no longer have clear images or memories to go with the feelings. As you extend compassion to yourself and your armor softens, earlier experiences of being separated from true self may come forward to be recognized. Perhaps even your initial experience of separation from true self will reveal itself for healing.

Remember that your hate need not
close you down; it can remind you of
compassion and give you the opportunity
to clear some powerful feelings.

Your way through the unbearable pain of hating is to know that, more than anything, you want to regain your connection to unlimited being. You want true self even more than you want revenge, even more than you want your "enemies" to finally see how wrong, bad, or flawed they have been. Your desire for reconnection with the unlimited love, peace, and divinity that you truly are becomes most important. This alignment of priorities brings you to a position of power; your energies are directed with true purpose.

You may find that your energy system is not quite strong enough to hold that set of aligned priorities for very long at a time. That's all right. The more you repeat the experience of choosing true self, the more your energy system adjusts and strengthens itself. Then it becomes easier to maintain the experience for longer periods.

Understand that if you have lived twenty or thirty or fifty years with a habit of going into war posture when you are threatened, your energy pattern is well-developed to support your being at war. It may take some time for your energy system to restructure itself to the pattern of compassion and forgiveness. In that period of transition, which could be days, weeks, months, or even years, be patient with yourself. The time it takes your system to restructure will ultimately enable you to hold the experience of true self and unlimited being more continuously in your daily life.

Be aware that your ego may periodically object to this focus on forgiveness and reconnection with true self. The ego, which has been conditioned to self-righteousness or self-pity, may still insist that other people be made to see what they did wrong, or be punished, or be shamed, or be made to apologize, and so on. There is no need to silence your ego; it is an expression of your personality and is, therefore, worthy of being heard. But you may want to remember that your ego's greatest skill is not in bringing you home to greater truth and inner connection.

Because of the various psychological and spiritual usages of the term "ego," you may tend to think of your ego as a problem, a self-centeredness, or, at best, something you must overcome if you want to attain spiritual enlightenment. I do not refer to ego in that way. For our purposes, ego is simply the part of your mind that adapted long ago to losing your connection to true self. It became your personality's leader in that state of loss and has been responsible for your survival in limited reality.

Everything your ego thinks and perceives is in the context of separation and limitation. To your ego, true self is not real. Therefore, desires and actions that come from your ego never fully take into account that unity and unlimited love are possible. In short, your ego can tell you how to operate in a limited world *without* your connection to true self; it cannot show you how to reconnect. For that you must extend beyond your ego and invite your true self to show you the way. Forgiving yourself in the midst of hate is a powerful invitation.

So you see, forgiveness begins primarily in your relationship with yourself. Empowering yourself with the gifts of your own heart frees you of injuries it seems others have brought you. As you receive your own forgiveness or compassion, forgiving others happens naturally as a side effect of healing yourself.

———————————◆———————————

Meditation

Forgiveness

1. Close your eyes, and breathe easily and fully. As you breathe, let each breath fill you with a feeling, image, or sense of love. Enjoy the love, and allow it to grow within you. . . .

2. When you are ready, think of someone whom you have difficulty forgiving. Imagine this person coming forward and facing you at a safe distance. Let yourself feel how uncomfortable it is for you to hold feelings of blame, hate, frustration, or resentment toward the person. . . .

3. As you face this person, make only the following change in the situation: breathe love into yourself again. This love is not necessarily for the other person; it is for you. You are being filled with the light of love, the feeling of love, the thought of love. . . . Each breath gives you more love for yourself, even as you remain in the presence of the other person. . . .

4. From this alignment with love, think or speak words like the following: "I give love and compassion to myself right now." "I allow my true self to fill me with its light." "I forgive myself for my pain and suffering. I allow myself to be healed by love."

5. Feel the meaning of your words take effect as you say them or think them. Stay with the feeling of love, compassion, forgiveness, or healing for as long as you like. . . .

6. Now let the other person fade, disappear, or walk out of your image. . . . When you are ready to come out of meditation, your compassion for yourself comes with you into the world. As you open your eyes, the love and healing remain; they are truly within you now.

◆

33

Anger

Your exploration of love will at some point bring you to anger's door. No matter how many techniques you learn for loving yourself and others, sooner or later you must make your peace with anger. Your challenge is to learn to find your way of receiving the glorious light of life even when you are angry.

There is nothing wrong with being angry. Your anger can give you important feedback about the events around you and when it is important to do something about them. But because anger is usually expressed in distorted and destructive ways, and because anger often activates the personality at the exclusion of the unconditionally loving self, many people feel that anger is not a "spiritual" experience.

Understand that spirit is in every thought and feeling you can have. Spirit is in every cell of your body and every aspect of your personality. You can never be truly separate from spirit because you are spirit. So, every experience, including anger, is spiritual and serves a high purpose.

At the personality level, it is important for you to deal with the specific issues that trigger your anger. Sometimes this will mean standing up for yourself in a conflict or a threatening situation. Other times you may need to assess whether your anger is really related to the situation that triggered it or is old patterning that no longer serves you. If you have trouble knowing how to take appropriate action with your anger (or with your response to someone else's), by all means get assistance from a wise and reliable source. There are excellent books as well as skilled therapists available to help you grow into a healthy relationship with anger. It is worth pursuing and is part of the life-long ritual of honoring and clearing your personality so it can serve you on your path of growth.

For now, let's leave the psychological aspects of anger as well as its appropriate expression. (These need to be explored in circumstances that give you the ongoing support you need.) Instead, let's focus on the energetic aspect of anger and how you can open to the vitality it carries.

There is vitality within all emotion;
this vitality is the birthright of every
being who comes into physical form.

When you allow yourself to have the vitality within your anger, you will find it easier to allow yourself to have everything else that you truly want in life. It all comes down to allowing the life force to flow through you.

Because vitality is the basic energy flow of life, it is what connects you to physical reality, literally giving you life and enabling you to be present and active in the physical world. Holding back or stopping your vitality would be foolish, ludicrous! Why would you want to stop the flow of energy that keeps you alive and sustains your very existence in physical form? Yet, when your anger is denied, your vitality is also denied. If you do not let your anger through in a clean, open, life-affirming way, it works against you, separating you energetically from the world you came here to embrace.

This does not mean that to allow yourself vitality you must always be angry. Vitality is experienced in a full range of other feelings and states of being as well. You have a wide repertoire! But by denying or withholding your anger you deny yourself a basic connection with life.

If anger seems negative to you, you are
probably thinking of distorted anger.

Understand that anger is not always rage and is not necessarily violent. Anger need not be misdirected or pent up or discharged in emotional attack. Pure anger is a feeling that creates a conduit for energy; it flushes the life force through your system. It can be as powerful as the force of love or joy in opening your heart and healing your body. Pure anger connects people rather than separates them, communicates rather than destroys.

Why, then, is anger so often experienced as negative and destructive? We live in a culture where the ego is separated from true self and relies heavily on the ability to be "in control." The prevailing pattern is to feel emotions only to the extent we can remain in control of them. This need for control prevents us from making peace with emotions that convey life force powerfully.

Because we are unaware that we are truly one with life force, life force seems separate from us and bigger than we are. So the power of life force, which we cannot control, is perceived as a threat to whatever control we may have established in life. Emotions, such as anger, that are natural conductors of raw, uncontrolled life force are feared and generally are not well managed.

Because we have been taught to distrust our anger rather than honor it and allow its flow, it frequently becomes distorted. As a culture we have worked so hard at controlling this emotion that we often mistake even the faintest feeling of anger for the need for greater control. Expressing our anger, then, can easily turn into a battle to control others or to keep from being controlled by them.

For example, you may have learned to fling your anger at others in an attempt to control them, the situation, or your vulnerability instead of allowing anger to show you how healing can take place. Or perhaps you keep your anger completely bottled up to ensure you don't use it destructively. When you resist or disallow anger, that energy doesn't go away. Because it must go somewhere, it is often rerouted into a less clear and less direct expression. It's quite likely that the energy of disowned anger is unconsciously turned inward and used against yourself.

You may have unknowingly adopted such a self-destructive emotional pattern early in life. Perhaps in your family no one tolerated being the recipient of your anger, so you learned not to express it directly to others. It may have been acceptable, however, for you to turn your anger against yourself through self-criticism or self-hatred. You may even have gotten the message that if you were angry at someone, you actually deserved to have something bad happen to you because of it. This conditioning could have set the pattern for the energy of your anger to come back to you in destructive ways.

Considering the narrow range of options the culture offers, it is natural that you may resist your anger as well as the anger of others. The irony is that in the fight to maintain control, you have forgotten anger's real purpose! You have forgotten that anger is an energy of communication and connection rather than of alienation and opposition. You have forgotten that anger is a powerful feeling that triggers your energy system to open more fully to life force. You have forgotten that being open to the flow of life force as it streams through your body and connects you with true self is what life is all about and is, therefore, more important than "winning" any battle.

*As you develop the ability to receive
the pure, vital energy in anger, you open
to a powerful new healing source.*

As the energy of creation, vital life force is the most profound healing energy there is. So in its pure form, anger is a healing energy rather than a destructive one. Because few people have learned to be open to and accepting of undistorted anger, few people realize the tremendous healing power it carries.

Exploring this element of anger requires that you hold a clear focus and pay attention. You need a strong, conscious commitment to self to stay present and follow through on the progression of feelings and experiences that will emerge. As you open to the pure life vitality in anger, you will find yourself beginning to open to pure experience at many other levels as well. Vitality links you to true self, and the effects of that connection are always far-reaching.

A primary step in opening to the vitality of anger is to notice that when you're angry, you have tremendous energy at your disposal and you have choice about how you direct it. You can use that energy to dam yourself up inside, deaden yourself, hold yourself back, think abusive thoughts about yourself, or send it out toward other people in similarly destructive ways. Or, you can receive the gift of vitality that comes with that emotion and be enlivened by it. That vitality then nourishes you, enriching your life and your relationships with other people.

Anger is an emotion and a physiological response in the body. Whether you use the emotion in a destructive way or a life-affirming way directly affects the chemistry of your body, which in turn enhances or diminishes your physical, mental, emotional, and energetic well-being. Your choice in interpreting and directing the energy of anger is what makes all the difference. If this choice is not made consciously, it happens unconsciously from your long held patterns of habit. Whichever way it occurs, your choice determines whether you move into increased experience of vibrant life or into depletion.

Underneath anger is usually a feeling of helplessness.

Even if you are not consciously in touch with it, that helplessness may cause you to overlook the true power you always have in anger: the power to choose life. You are probably not trained to recognize such power. Few parents say to their angry children, "You are angry. It's a strong feeling, and I want you to notice how much power you have. You have a choice to use this power in a life-affirming way. How can you do that? What would be a good way? Talk to me about it, and I will help you." But if you did not get this support from a parent, you can learn to give it to yourself.

When you feel angry, stop briefly and take a few deep breaths to become present with yourself. Consciously notice that, in spite of any distressing emotion that may be circulating through your system, you are at a point of power. You have the power of choice.

As you focus on this thought, you may discover some resistance to claiming your power when you are angry. Your habituated reaction to anger may seem to have a life of its own and may be difficult to stop, even for just a moment. As impractical and uncomfortable as it may be, unconsciously you may also be attached to the familiarity of your old pattern. Watch for your resistance. It is natural. Notice it and then ask yourself, "Do I want to go with the resistance this time and keep the old pattern, or do I want to make a change and remember that I am at a point of power here?"

Of course, the power is not power over the person or situation that is the focus for your upset feelings. It is the power of being able to choose how much affirmation of life you will carry in your body. That is far more important than any issue you are likely to be angry about.

Because the cultural patterning
of anger is so strong, it is easy
to get stuck arguing the issues and trying
to gain or maintain control.

Imagine, for example, that you are in an argument with someone and your temper flares. You are tempted to fall into your old pattern of using your anger to intimidate, belittle, or find fault with your adversary to win the argument and, therefore, avoid the feeling of being defeated yourself. Or perhaps your tendency is to pretend you are not angry, to sulk, or to make the other person feel guilty so they will retreat. In these cases, the pure energy of your anger is misdirected, which short circuits your flow of vitality. In this compromised state, you have literally forgotten your source of true well-being, and this is a very real loss to you. Is gaining control in an argument worth the cost of diminished vitality to your own system?

Learning to give anger its natural, direct expression, which includes giving up control over others, allows the pure vitality of anger to stream through all levels of your being, nourishing and revitalizing every cell of your body. This in itself is one definition of "winning" in an argument. For example, if the other person's opinion or decision prevails at a practical level, you can have the personal victory of walking away with vibrant life that is not dependent on the outcome of the argument.

This certainly does not mean that you must always make an either/or choice between inner, personal victory and outer effectiveness. You need not retreat or be passive in a conflict to maintain your energetic integrity. In fact, staying open to life force can increase your ability to be centered and empowered within yourself, to hold your ground, and to communicate with the strength or passion you truly feel.

What you may need to do, however, is start noticing your misdirection of anger as it happens and then give yourself some new options. Learning new techniques for healthy containment and expression of anger can help tremendously. Also, choosing vitality often in your life and becoming familiar with what it feels like in a variety of situations can establish a recognizable base of well-being, which you can return to when you become angry.

The bottom line is that sometimes your expression of anger will get you the outer results you want and sometimes it will not. Yet, all experience has one basic purpose: to bathe you with unlimited life. When you accept this truth, revitalizing yourself by being fully open to receiving life force becomes your highest priority. You can then choose your response in every situation based on what would enhance your flow of true vitality and well-being rather than diminish it.

As you live with this clear, aligned intention, other people's ways of dealing with anger may become less relevant as models for your own behavior. You are unplugging from the culturally held consciousness about anger. While the cultural beliefs still include the unconscious assumption that anger equals an inner loss or death, you are beginning to use anger as a vehicle for vibrant life.

At the moment when they are at their own point of power, most people have no idea of the magnificent choice they face.

Given conscious choice, most people would choose increased vibrancy; yet relatively few actually realize that their anger can take them to such an experience. Without a greater awareness, cultural habit prevails and people tend to let anger shut down their flow of vibrant life force. The body and energy system know the difference between being life enhanced or life deprived; even subtle restriction of the life force is recognized as movement toward deadness. To the degree they shut down, most people automatically react to anger as though it threatens their survival. Ironically, it is the act of shutting down that is the true threat. Without understanding this dynamic, people respond to anger, their own as well as other people's, with fear.

Unplugging from this cultural pattern means a profound change in your life; again it is natural that your personality may display its resistance. If that happens, it may help to stop, take a deep breath, and then briefly lend a compassionate ear to the resistance. Hear what the voice of resistance has to say, and take notes for it. Write a few words, perhaps even two or three sentences, to capture the message. This allows the resistance to be expressed and then released onto paper.

If the resistance returns, gently repeat the procedure as needed. Important information about your inner process and your personality's needs may be revealed to you in this way. By expressing, hearing, and releasing the resistance, you are redirecting its flow. It no longer operates in a closed circuit, keeping you stuck. It is being trained to inform you and then pass through, leaving you free to make new choices.

Remember, resistance to empowering change comes from the element of personality that does not yet know you can have more fulfillment than you have had in the past. It operates from habit and limitation and tries to protect you.

As a creation of your own unlimited spirit, your personality is worthy of being loved and honored; you just don't have to believe it as you once did.

Honor your personality by hearing its concerns; then take another deep breath and go back to your point of power. Feel your anger and consider your choice consciously. "I feel a powerful energy moving through me. I can choose to let it enliven me or shut me down. Vitality or deadness. Vibrant life or slow depletion. Which do I choose?"

When you are at this point of considering aliveness or depletion, it may sometimes feel impossible to choose life. The old conditioning may still seem too strong. Your inner self-critic may interpret this as a sign of personal failure on your part. It may say that you are a weak person, that you are not enlightened enough, that you do not deserve to feel good, or something equally deflating. The content of these critical messages is usually not true and does not matter anyway. What is more helpful than evaluating your self-worth is simply being honest with yourself about when you are choosing the vitality of life and when you are choosing nonlife. Honest observation is all that is needed.

When you choose nonlife, you are not making a bad choice. You are simply doing what you are doing. You can still accept yourself. In fact, you can still full-heartedly love yourself, even though you may wish you could have made a different choice. Noticing with conscious awareness which choice you are making while giving yourself acceptance, support, and love in that moment is in itself significant empowerment.

The good news is that you are all right regardless of the choice you make. There are no good choices or bad choices in life. There are ones that bring you into greater direct experience of vital life force and choices that diminish that experience, but there is no good and bad. All the choices you make are done with unlimited blessing from unlimited beings. And in all those choices, absolute love is still the core of who you truly are, regardless of what you experience in the moment when you take your action.

There is nothing wrong with you when you make a choice that restricts the flow of vitality through your being. In fact, giving yourself acceptance and love in that situation nourishes your system and lays new circuitry that will enable you to make a more life-affirming decision the next time, or the next, or the next. If you catch yourself being unable to direct your anger in a new, life-affirming way, then breathe, remember the love that you are, and pat yourself on the back for being an excellent human being who is pursuing the exploration of limitation.

If you strongly believe that anger is destructive, it may be difficult to allow yourself to open to it, even though you know that anger carries vital healing force. Be very patient, gentle, and loving with yourself and take the process slowly. If you are at risk of being overwhelmed, or have reason to fear your patterns of response to anger, or need new input to develop healthy expressions for this powerful emotion, support yourself by getting qualified outside help.

Anger is not always comfortable, but it is far more comfortable when it is allowed to move through as the vitality of life rather than resisted as though it is something negative or dangerous. Anger is dangerous if you use it against yourself or others. It can be healing for yourself and others when it is allowed to flow through freely and naturally.

When you can allow yourself to feel anger in a way that does not close you off to yourself or others, but instead opens you to the very life force that feeds and nurtures you, you will not fear anger so much. In opening to the vitality of life within anger, you are opening to true self while becoming more present in your physical body. You are bringing the truth of your spirit into physical experience, which is the essential purpose of your journey into form.

◆

Attunement
Staying Aware in Anger

You are setting new patterns, which require repetition. New experience has to be real to the body before the automatic emotional responses can genuinely change. During the time of repatterning, staying conscious and witnessing your choices will help. When anger surfaces, you can go through the following steps:

1. Feel the vibrant energy.
2. Recognize that you are at a point of power.
3. Notice that you have a choice to enhance or restrict your flow of life force.
4. Become clear on what action will best support your well-being.
5. Stay aware as you take whatever action you choose.
6. Give yourself acceptance and notice how it feels.

◆

Meditation
Healing Through Anger

The following meditation can give you practice in shifting your patterns of energetic response to anger. You can experiment with it in small increments of perhaps five to fifteen minutes every few days or weeks. It's best to choose times when you are not lost in overwhelming anger to begin with so that you have some range within which to maneuver. Don't move so far into anger that you lose natural control. You'll want to be able to guide yourself in and out of the anger gently. Consider having someone else with you to support or guide you until you're comfortable doing it yourself.

(Note: If while doing this visualization you sense that your feelings of anger may become too uncomfortable or intense, simply stop. Open your eyes, breathe gently and easily for a few moments, and bathe yourself in love. Give yourself compassion for having gone as far as you were ready to go. Honor your limits and do not push yourself.)

1. Begin by imagining a situation when you were angry. You may remember a real-life situation, or you may make one up. Give yourself a few moments to let the situation form in your imagination. . . . Let yourself feel some of the anger—not enough to overwhelm you, but just enough to remember how anger feels. . . .

2. Also imagine that your purpose is not to change the situation that makes you angry or to change anyone else's mind or actions. Instead, your purpose is simply to allow the vitality of life to flow through your body and your energy system along with the anger. Vitality is the main experience, and the anger is just the

medium for it. Gently allow your energy system to open more so that vitality streams through you. . . .

3. You can feel the anger, yet you don't have to put it into action or words. You don't have to fight. You don't have to convince or interact with anyone. You are simply in that situation to experience the positive flow of vitality that anger carries. . . .

4. There is plenty of space for the vitality to move through your system. This energy, or life force, has a natural wisdom of its own. As it flows, it feeds and nourishes every cell in our body. It brings life and radiance into your being. Absorb and accept this healing force. . . .

5. Now imagine that the angry situation you were facing disappears into light. All stress disappears with it. The light lingers long enough to cleanse you of any residue of anger, conflict, or discomfort, leaving you washed with radiant vitality and well-being.

After you feel familiar with this meditation and are comfortable guiding yourself through it, the next step is to allow yourself to open consciously to this process while you are really in a situation of anger. It can all be done in a minute or two—or even in a few seconds, if necessary. Pause for a moment, take a few deep breaths, and with those breaths gently open to the vitality in anger. Allow the flow through your system to be as natural as possible. Give the vitality plenty of room. Let yourself feel this positive life force moving through your body and going directly into your tissues. Know that you are experiencing a healing energy that can show you how to constructively deal with the situation.

◆

Part VII
Sexuality

The Embodiment of Spirit

34

Sexual Energy and Life Force

Sexual energy connects us to physical reality in much the same way a tree's roots secure it to the earth. It is our grounding force. Through our sexual energy we embrace the earth and, at the same time, receive nourishing earth energy that cannot be received in any other way. So, just as a very tall and ancient tree would never choose to sever its roots, we would never benefit from stopping our flow of sexual energy. Sexual energy that is allowed its natural flow and is directed in a life-enhancing manner always strengthens our systems at every level.

You can think of sexuality as vitality that you bring with you from spirit into physical form. Your spirit has a certain range of vibration that is specifically yours. As your spirit comes into physical form, that vibration comes into harmony with the range of vibration that is physical-level consciousness at the time of your life on earth. That is your vitality of life. Your ability to continuously channel this vitality through your physical being is what keeps you alive in physical form.

The vitality of life can be felt, seen, and experienced by those who are sensitive to it. A tree has the vitality of life flowing through it. A cloud has the vitality of life flowing through it. Air, as unformed as it seems to be, has the vitality of life flowing through it. This is an energy that every thing and every being in physical form have in common.

The ultimate purpose of sexual energy
is to unite spirit with physical form.

Sexual energy functions primarily to bring you intimacy with physical reality and to give your spirit a way to energetically embrace the physical world. One vehicle for this spiritual purpose is sexual interaction between people. Through sex it is possible to interact on three levels: physical body to physical body, energy system to energy system, and spirit to spirit.

Western culture puts tremendous focus on physical sexual interaction, but it does not teach about the need to experience your spirit's connection with physical reality. This over-focus on the physical at the expense of the energetic and spiritual gives an incompleteness or imbalance to many people's sexual experiences. Their response to this dilemma may be to over-compensate through physical sexuality for their need (which is unconscious and unmet) to connect at the energetic and spiritual levels.

In such cases people may have an urgency or addictiveness about physical sexual interaction. At a subconscious or unconscious level there will be an unease, perhaps even a panic, when there is not regular sexual activity. For them physical sex is not a vehicle, but is instead a substitute, for linking spirit with physical reality. Their spiritual relationship with physical form is tenuous and is threatened when sex becomes unavailable. Without sexual activity their sense of self becomes less "real," less grounded, more uncomfortable.

Sexuality is a conduit for the vitality of life in a very focused and powerful way. As is the case with all powerful feelings, restricting the flow of sexual energy restricts the flow of vitality and the connection to physical reality. Ironically, along with the culture's overfocus on physical sex, there is also strong conditioning to squelch or distort sexual energy and, therefore, vitality. People who have been particularly susceptible to that conditioning are living in pain at a very deep level.

Numerous influences may have caused you to close off to your sexuality. Many beliefs based on morality or religion say that sexual activity is not appropriate and must be withheld or at least limited. This is often interpreted to mean that sexuality at all levels must automatically be denied, distorted, or withheld. Yet, it is possible to restrict sexual *activity* without restricting sexual *energy*. With a clear focus of awareness, the energy can flow unimpeded regardless of whether you choose to act on it. (Understand that sexual energy refers to an energy or vibration, which is far more subtle than a feeling. Sexual energy is technically not the same thing as sexual feelings, although it may be through your sexual feelings that you are most aware of this energy.)

Many people coming into spiritual awakening experience sexuality as a distraction from spiritual growth. Some insist that anyone serious about spiritual growth must be celibate to make true progress. Spirituality and sexuality are held as a duality, presenting an either/or conflict: you can have spirituality or sexuality, but not the two together.

Let's look at duality for a moment. Either/or assumptions are limiting because they deny all-inclusive experiences. They exclude anything but the two polarized sides of the issue. Such exclusion makes it difficult for altogether new information or perspective to make its way into dualistic reality.

Does this mean that duality is wrong? Not at all. Remember, there is nothing inferior about limitation. In fact, we have all come into physical form to explore duality precisely because it is so limiting. As part of our greater investigation, taking on dualistic perception and judgment is a perfect way to study limitation firsthand.

Some people seem to go through their lives perceiving reality only in terms of limitation, shutting out all ideas or experiences that may broaden their awareness. Even though it can be frustrating to be around those people if we want them to be different, their lives may be profoundly productive in ways that we—or even they—do not consciously recognize.

Such an orientation to limitation may allow those people to hold a strong, unwavering focus on a specific stratum of life experience, enabling them to move into it far more deeply and thoroughly than would be likely if they were open to other possibilities. It is a form of specialization. By using limitation (and specifically, perhaps, duality) to keep their focus, they are able to do intense, precision work in the exploration of physical consciousness.

Now, regarding sexuality. There is also a belief in the spiritual value of celibacy that does not come from dualistic conflict, but naturally emerges as an individual is ready to explore it. The catalyst for such celibacy may be a profound spiritual experience or exposure to a specific spiritual teaching. Or, it may simply begin with an inner knowing that comes in the progression of awakening for that person's consciousness.

So, it's clear there are people who have chosen, for any number of reasons, to abstain from sexual activity for the pursuit of spirituality. And there are people who have chosen to pursue sexual activity along with spiritual learning. Both choices have a place in spiritual growth and can be used as a vehicle for transformation. Neither choice is by itself better than the other. What matters most is making the choice that is genuinely right for you and that nourishes your connection with both spirit and physical form.

35

Sexual Activity

For those who do allow sexual activity to be a part of their daily living (or at least intend it to be), let's explore the blending of sexuality and spirituality. As you may have found, sexuality can be a distraction from spiritual awareness simply because of the powerful physical sensations that go along with sexual feelings. There is nothing wrong with forgetting spirituality by being distracted into sexuality. But if you intend to use sexuality to align even more deeply and completely with the spirit of self and others, you may want to experiment with the following shift of awareness.

Vitality flows through the circuitry of your energy system, which is very closely aligned with your physical body. As your body is physically stimulated, the energy system is stimulated as well. This energy connects your spirit to physical reality through your body. Not only does sexual feeling awaken your body, but it also stimulates the energy system and spirit to vibrate with life.

While you are engaged in sexual feelings
it is possible to expand your awareness
to include not only physical sensations
but also energy vibration
and presence of spirit.

The following four steps may help you focus on a progressive transtion for this expansion of awareness. They are intended to be done while making love, although it is also possible to do them without physical contact that is sexually stimulating. (Indeed, these steps are a form of lovemaking in themselves, with or without physical sex.) If you do follow these steps during physical lovemaking, you may find your focus sometimes being stretched to hold physical, energetic, and spiritual awareness all at once. That stretch is an important part of your growth, so give yourself the time you need for it. You may want to have an agreed-upon signal that you or your partner can use whenever one of you needs to pause or slow down the physical activity in order to reattune your inner focus.

It is quite all right if you do not fully complete all four steps in the first session! Sensing energy during sex is in itself a huge

leap for most people. Do not worry if you find yourself needing several sessions for each step. Many people spend their
whole lives working with these techniques. Remember that
this growth is progressive and will have its greatest effects over
time. Also, when you work with such subtle levels of awareness, the feedback is not always definite; you may often be
doing better than you know. Be patient and loving with yourself and your partner, and enjoy the process.

◆

Attunement
Spiritual Awareness in Lovemaking

1. *Your Energy.* As your energy system vibrates in physical lovemaking, there is a change in color in your
   energy field within and around your body. Allow
   yourself to tune into your energy and explore any
   sense of vibration or color. Ask yourself something
   like, "Where do I feel my energy moving? What is the
   vibration like? What color do I sense my energy to
   be?" Maybe just thinking the word "energy" will be
   enough to cue yourself into that focus.

   Your sense of energy may be very localized or it
   may be more general; either is fine. This is subtle work,
   so you may find that you get more information through
   inner image than through actual physical sensation.
   Follow your awareness and open to whatever is there.

   When you are able to sense your energy along
   with your physical experience of sex, you are ready to
   add step 2.

2. *Your Partner's Energy.* As your energy system vibrates and the life force flows through, your partner's
   energy system is automatically stimulated as well.

This is a very deep communication between the two of you that goes beyond words and physical touch. It is an intimate connection from energy system to energy system. As you allow yourself to be aware of your own energy response, you will more easily be able to sense your partner's energy, too. You can expand your awareness to include your partner by asking yourself, "Where do I sense energy vibrating or moving in my partner? What color or feeling is that energy?"

Give yourself plenty of time to practice and explore these two steps. When you are comfortable sensing or perceiving energy in both yourself and your partner along with feeling the physical sexual sensations, you are ready to look to the spirit.

3. *Your Spirit.* This step is about sensing and aligning with your spirit in the midst of your physical and energetic sexual experiences. Your spirit is always with you and within you. Allow your awareness to expand to discover its presence. As you tune in, ask a question such as, "What sense or feeling or image do I have of my spirit right now?" Or, simply think the word "spirit."

Through the progression from physical body to energy system to spirit, each level is more subtle, more refined. Because of the subtlety of the spirit level, at first you may not have a conscious sense of what your spirit is like. With practice you will be able to tune into it more easily. Your sense of spirit will be your own—not necessarily like anyone else's—and may change as your awareness grows.

4. *Your Partner's Spirit.* As your connection with your spirit becomes more natural and real to you, an

interesting thing will happen. You will find yourself spontaneously becoming more aware of your partner's spirit. Because your own spirit's state is unity, its natural tendency is to experience true connection with others. The intimacy you and your partner have already developed at this point of your lovemaking will allow your spirit to show you your partner's spirit easily. This can be very subtle, so if you're not certain it's happening you may need to think a trigger thought such as "unity" or your partner's name.

───────────────── ◆ ─────────────────

Through this progression of steps, your sexual interaction with your partner grows. It starts as physical body to physical body, continues as energy system to energy system, and then expands to include the refined truth of spirit to spirit. Spirit to spirit connection is the deepest intimacy people can experience. It is an exciting discovery and a true joy, like opening to the greatest freedom possible.

Beings of spirit clamor to come into physical form for the tremendous exploration and discovery that are offered in limitation. Yet those who are here often feel restricted by this realm and when they are able to experience something that takes them beyond physical form, they are ecstatic. That transcendence and joy are possible in spiritual sex. Those who have experienced it would call it absolute union with their sexual partner. There is a merging, a unity of two beings becoming one, that is a return to the unlimitedness you once knew.

The deep satisfaction and joy of being in union with your partner is very similar to feeling unconditional love. From that state you are able to see your partner with purity. There is no barrier, no judgment, no separation—just true love and an intuitive understanding of how deeply you are connected.

So, there is room for spirituality and sexuality together. The one can enhance the other; when you move toward unity with another person you always learn something about the truth of your greater being.

At a deep level of spirit you already know your unlimited truth, but the challenge is in bringing that knowing into your experience of physical life. It's one thing to know your true self when you are focused in the realm of spirit, perhaps in the sleep state, in meditation, or in death. But it's another thing to bring that awareness through when you're very focused in the physical.

What better way to have your attention focused in physical reality than to have it focused in your body? And what more effective stimulus is there for bringing your awareness into your body than sexuality? Your body is your spirit's representative in physical consciousness. It is not only a vehicle to enable your spirit to engage with the physical world, but your entire relationship with physical reality and physical consciousness is played out in your body.

When you experience unity through sexuality, your body participates directly with unlimited spirit.

In transcendent sexual union, the experience of spirit imprints deeply into your body at a cellular and chemical level. Your body and energy system are stimulated in a way that very slightly, but profoundly, shifts the physical and energetic patterning at a subtle, core level. This shift grounds the spiritual experience throughout your being, integrating it into your body and personality and making it part of the reality from which you now consciously operate. This integration strengthens your ability to create and contain more expanded spiritual experiences in the future.

36

Celibacy

You can explore the dramatic power of vital life force through sexual energy without actively being involved in sexual interaction. Actually, to say "physical" sexual interaction would be more appropriate because there is always sexual interaction taking place at an energy level, not only from person to person but among all living things. For example, as you look at a tree, the sexual energy of your being, which knows no boundaries, reaches out and interacts with the tree. Your vitality, your physical life force, does not shut off from anything or anyone. It radiates outward and makes contact with life in all forms.

If you have chosen celibacy, you can still open to sexual energy. You do not need to fear it, control it, or reject it. Allow yourself to view sexual energy as simply the life force connecting your spirit to physical reality. To put a block in the way of that life force would hold you back from being fully present in the physical world.

If you watch closely you may find that you do not always want to be fully present in the physical world. You may fear that the density of experiences in the physical realm, especially emotions or intense physical sensations, restricts your spiritual connection. Yet whatever the resistance, the pain, the difficulty about being in physical reality may be, stopping the flow of vital life energy only weakens your ability to deal with it.

Many people assume that if they can subdue the physical life force within their being and crank up the spiritual energy, they will be more aligned, more pure, and more safe from physical reality. Instead, subduing or resisting their life force only creates an imbalance that makes them weaker and less stable. You have come into physical form to explore it, to embrace it, to be in it and, from there, to bring the knowing of spirit into physical consciousness. You cannot complete this progression without being physically present. So do whatever you can to allow the vital life force to flow more cleanly. This vital energy nourishes you and creates a stronger body, a more vibrant energy field, and a deeper connection with physical reality and planet Earth. Simply holding the view of sexual energy as the vital life force may already be a powerful shift for you.

> *Sexual energy enables you*
> *to be fully alive and spiritually open*
> *to the physical plane.*

If you are intentionally celibate, are simply not in a sexual relationship, or for some other reason choose not to physically act on your sexual feelings, you can consciously choose to open to sexual energy whenever you feel it moving in your body. Imagine it as a circuit of life force flowing through your body and your energy system, keeping you alive and maintaining vibrant balance. Then direct that energy to any area of your body that seems to ask for strengthening or healing.

Sexual energy is a powerful healer when it is allowed its free flow and when it is recognized for what it truly is. Because it is the energetic force of life connecting your spirit to physical form, it is the most balanced, most aligned physical energy you can experience. It has unlimited power to create or heal at the physical level.

Now remember the love that you are. In "Self-Love" we talked about this love as also being the life force, the essence of all things, your link to unlimitedness. Imagine the benefit of consciously attuning to sexual energy and essence love together. When combined, these energies can bring the healing of unlimitedness and love directly into your physical body.

Because sexual energy carries the essence vitality of spirit and is the physicalized energy of unity, it has the power to burst through habituated beliefs in limitation and separation. It brings the reality of your true nature into the cells of your body and into your perceptions of the world around you.

————————————— ◆ —————————————

Attunement
Sexual Energy and Healing

1. Imagine your sexual energy as coming from your spirit. It is a circuit of life force flowing through your body and your energy system, keeping you alive and maintaining vibrant balance. . . .

2. Imagine the love that is the essence of your being emerging (perhaps from your heart) and joining the sexual energy as it circulates. . . .

3. Feel the pleasure and well-being this energy combination creates in your body. . . .

4. Direct this energy to any areas of your body that particularly need attention or revitalization—perhaps a sore throat, aching joints, muscles that are tense. . . .

5. If you are familiar with chakras, the energy centers of the body, you can direct healing energy to any chakras you want to balance. . . .

6. When you are done, take three deep breaths, and bring your awareness back to your surroundings.

————————————— ◆ —————————————

Attunement
Sexual Energy and Unity

1. Be aware of sexual energy as it moves through your body. . . .

2. Be aware that you do not intend to put this energy into sexual activity; instead, allow yourself to see how

it unites you with all things and all beings. . . . Let yourself imagine that your sexual energy radiates outward from your body through the air, connecting you with everything and everyone in its path. . . . If you are indoors, let your inner sight show you how this subtle radiance streams from your being and blends into the wall, the floor, the furniture. . . . If you are outside, witness your connection with the trees, the cars, the people, the street, the sky. . . .

3. Notice that all physical creation, nature made or human made, is united by this powerful energy flow. . . . Some people see this connection as threads of energy or light or as color shining forth. Others do not have a visual image at all but simply sense the unity as they focus on it. Be open to whatever your own perception may be. . . .

4. When you are ready, take three breaths and release the experience of unity. Let your normal level of perception return.

◆

Part VIII

Living the Split

---◆---

Redefining Destiny

37

Heeding the Call

Conscious and fulfilling awareness of true self is calling to you from every cell in your body. It is your destiny making itself known, and it pulls you along the track of your life. Sometimes you feel the pull and follow it easily and naturally. That is bliss. Other times there is surprising effort and the pain of bruised shins as you bump into a myriad of half-buried obstacles restricting your path. Then there is the occasion when your way is so thoroughly blocked it seems you cannot make passage at all.

The obstructions in your path are creations of your limited beliefs and expectations of reality, which you have been carrying around with you for more years than you probably know. As they spring out and take form in your life, you meet them straight on, and they get in your way. If you continue believing in their existence, you struggle with them. You plot and plan your way around them. But limitations are persistent, and they pop up over and over again. As long as you hold them in your identity, you will encounter them in your path.

But take heart. Remember that unlimited life is at the core of everything, including your limitation. Although the obstacles in your path may seem solely like untimely impediments to your progress forward, they are also markers placed at points of power. You can claim this power by shifting your awareness and recognizing the existence of something greater than the limitation you are tripping over.

Something greater, in this case, is choice. You have choice. You can choose to continue in your previous habituated pattern, or you can choose to surrender to unlimited self to create your path anew. In this framework, consider that your destiny may be a pull rather than a plan, a process rather than an outcome, a matter of following the vibrancy of life force rather than being in the right place at the right time doing the right thing.

This is a destiny that has no particular form and that, in fact, is not dependent on specific events or situations for its expression. There is no fixed map with a set path you are to follow to make your life worthwhile, and there are no concrete ways to measure such things as success or failure. In such a reality, destiny is less about the "proper" unfolding of your life and more about the innate unfolding of your being.

Certainly, as your being unfolds and you open to unlimitedness, the forms in your life will be touched and reshaped. In fact, the impulse to follow destiny's call will surface in every aspect of your life sooner or later and can prompt you to want to make significant changes. Yet, do not confuse the changes that occur with destiny itself.

When you are following unlimited source,
you are adapting to a deep rhythm
of movement and transformation that
may be foreign to your personality.
At times your personality may holler
that the rhythm is too fast and,
at others, may whine and complain
that it is painfully slow.

Your life changes may begin with a feeling of dissatisfaction. It may be dissatisfaction with your work, your relationships, or any area of your life that involves your self-expression or way of relating to the world. There is a feeling that you want deeper fulfillment in the situation and want to be able to express or give more of who you truly are. The need to transform the current situation, or create a new one altogether, challenges you to continue drawing on deeper inner resources as you make your way.

Because large numbers of people are finding themselves at precisely this type of crossroad in respect to their work, let's use work as the example in this chapter. Perhaps career is not the area that concerns you, but you long for a deeper, more expansive relationship, a more compatible circle of friends, or a new creative outlet. The information in this section can be applied to a variety of areas in your life where you feel the pull toward expanded change that has not yet fully manifested.

If work is your area of focus, perhaps you are yearning for a job that allows you to express more fully who you are and to make a direct, perceivable contribution to the world. This yearning can become a passion. You may sense your greater potential flowing through your body so strongly that it feels uncomfortable because you don't yet have the appropriate action for releasing it into the world. You are so ready to find your true work that you are about to pop, but you may not even know yet what the form of that work is. Months can go by without your getting any clearer about it. Still, the yearning and readiness, your greater destiny, continue to pull on you.

At such times, the inner readiness to move into a new level of unlimited living appears to outpace what is actually happening in your outer life. This incongruity between the inner and outer realities is one of many possible variations of the split we discussed in "Journey into Form." Remember that the split is the gap in the personality's awareness between the experience of limitation and the greater reality of unlimited being. In this case you are witnessing it as the gap between your increasing inner awareness of unlimitedness and the circumstances in your life that still feel limiting.

In this version of the split, your job seems too limited to be a fulfilling expression for your greater self. As time passes, you may feel more expanded in your personal life yet even more empty and frustrated at work. Efforts to discover your new work may be unfruitful. You feel that you are spinning your wheels. Because you do not yet really know where you are going, it is understandable that you do not feel you are progressing in measurable ways.

After still more effort and frustration, you may begin turning your energy against yourself with self-sabotaging thoughts: "Something is wrong with me or I would have found my new work by now." "I am not trying hard enough." "I am not clear enough." "I should be more spiritual." "I should be more practical." In short, you have interpreted the existence of the split to mean that you are personally flawed in some way.

You may even choose the flip side of that interpretation. Instead of being antagonistic to self, you may decide that the flaw is outside yourself. "My problem exists because the world is not ready for what I have to offer." "Society is filled with density and limitation." "People's minds are closed. The world is not structured to allow people like me to make our contribution."

Both interpretations are based on the assumption that there is a flaw somewhere, and usually the flaw is not one you can fix. The effect is the same regardless of whether you perceive the flaw as being within you or outside you; you are stymied by it. This adds a sense of inadequacy or incapacitation to the frustration you already feel. Clearly, a new option for relating to the situation is needed.

Although your personality will be searching, perhaps in frantic exasperation, for new outer action to take, the most powerful thing you can do at this point may simply be to accept that you are in the split and become more consciously present within it. There are two basic steps for beginning this acceptance.

◆

Attunement
Accepting the Split

1. First, take some quiet time and attune to the greater potential you sense growing within. Feel it as it rises from your depths and fills you, streaming through every cell in your body. Notice how ready this energy is to go out into the world and carry the expansiveness and vitality of your true spirit into new work. Feel it as a passion, and cherish it.

2. Then, whenever you recognize that the outer reality has not yet changed to match your inner readiness, also take time to notice how that feels to you. Feel the difference between your expansive inner readiness and the restriction that is still present in your outer life. Do not try to minimize the tension or discomfort of being caught in the split. Stay with yourself in it. Let the full spectrum of the experience be real.

◆

Making time for this awareness is important. It may be your habit, as it is most people's, to try to race through the split as quickly as possible, minimizing its effect. Your automatic reaction may be to rev up your energy and, using all the effort you can muster, attempt a flying leap across the split to the other side, where you hope your new work will be waiting. This exertion is an attempt to avoid the discomfort of living with the split.

You cannot successfully cross the split that way. You will find yourself stopped in the middle time and time again. Ironically, this is to your benefit.

As you resist the split and its discomfort,
you resist some aspect of yourself that
knows it needs to be included in your
move forward into more expansive living.

You continue to stop because the aspect of self that waits in the split is worth stopping for. It needs to be held close to your heart and carried with you into the creation of your new life.

One way to extend friendship to this sometimes elusive aspect of yourself is to settle into the split for a while and feel what it is like. When you quit trying to leap the split and instead allow yourself to be in it, you are no longer resisting what is happening in the present in an effort to move ahead. Instead, you are surrendering to the present and finding out what it can contribute to your journey. This makes all the difference.

It also changes your immediate goal. You still want your true work, of course; that intention need not weaken. Yet the primary goal now becomes simply being with whatever is revealing itself right now. In this surrender, you notice the aliveness of your intention to find right work, and you also allow the discomfort of holding potential that has not yet come through into manifestation in the external world. You feel the split, which is preparation for gathering power.

38

Gathering Power

Spending time consciously in the split gives you the opportunity to face the blank slate of Not Knowing, which some people call "the void." Not Knowing is an important—and powerful—ally. You have undoubtedly already sensed its power, but you may have been frightened of it and may have fled. Without understanding how to let it serve you, it is easy to fear Not Knowing as something that will weaken you and keep you from gaining clarity about your path.

Fear of Not Knowing may be part of what motivated you to continue trying to leap over the split. You may have resisted and avoided Not Knowing, assuming that giving in to it would leave you even more disoriented and lost than ever. When you are already frustrated or scared because you do not know what your new work is to be or how to find it, moving into a state of knowing even less may seem like the wrong direction entirely.

Not Knowing is not a lack of ideas. It is a clear, pure, natural state of awareness that transcends personality and connects you with unlimited possibility. Fortunately, Not Knowing does not go away just because you don't recognize its value; it continues to offer itself. Yet, if you remain unaware of what it offers, you will continue resisting it and trying to fill its apparent emptiness. What will you try to fill it with? Knowing, of course.

> *When you fear Not Knowing, your*
> *natural defense is to try to know.*

You attempt to fill the Not Knowing with thoughts and ideas that you hope will get you to your new work. Personality is uncomfortable with open-ended questions and soothes itself by coming up with answers. Similarly, it is uncomfortable with the apparent emptiness of the split and tries to fill it in with tangibles. Personality believes that the way to find your new work is to stay in control, in this case to "know" your way there. It is not aware of how much more empowering and enriching it can be to "not know" your way there.

Not Knowing is a powerful state of being that transcends the thoughts and ideas generated by your intellect. Remember that intellect is based in the personality, which can create only according to the limitation it has already known. In your longing for true work, you are asking for an experience that goes beyond what has previously been your norm. To find it, you must open to a state of awareness that goes beyond what you have previously known. Ironically, one way to go beyond what you have known is to go into Not Knowing; there you are wide open.

Personality's knowing automatically
screens out possibilities that are
unfamiliar. Not Knowing does not limit
you to the possibilities your intellect can
create or your personality can plan;
instead you are open to the unlimited.

The yearning to find your true work (or relationship or creativity) is a variation on the desire for true self and is, therefore, another pure state. Allowing true yearning and Not Knowing, two essence energies, to meet and flow together creates the beginning of something new and more expanded. It is not so much the marriage of true yearning and knowing, but the marriage of true yearning and Not Knowing that yields the greatest possibility.

–––––––––––––––––––– ◆ ––––––––––––––––––––

Meditation

Yearning and Not Knowing

1. Close your eyes and allow your breath to take you deep into self. Follow a few breaths into your throat area. . . . Follow a few breaths into your heart area. . . . Follow a few breaths into your belly. . . .

2. As you continue to breathe gently and easily into deeper self, allow your yearning to surface. . . . You

may feel your yearning passionately or you may barely
feel it at all; it makes no difference. It is not the sensation that is important. It is your intent. When your
intent is to allow your yearning to surface, it will happen whether you feel it or not. . . .

3. Continue to sense the yearning as it is. . . . Now also
sense the Not Knowing, as though you are silently
inviting it to present itself, too. . . .

4. Not Knowing may appear as a blank screen, an empty
hole, a beautiful light, or as something else. It may
even come as nothing at all: no image or feeling or
sense of anything. Open to it in whatever way it presents itself. . . .

5. Allow the yearning and Not Knowing to spend time
with you together. . . . Breathe gently and easily into
the yearning and Not Knowing, allowing yourself to
trust their presence. . . .

6. When you are ready to come out of meditation, turn
your awareness to your whole body, noticing how it
feels from head to toe. . . . Then slowly stretch, and
open your eyes.

◆

39

Empowering Your Speech

Everything you say affects your consciousness, either affirm-
ing or changing your habits of thought. When your statements
allow room for new and fulfilling possibilities, you affirm your

true self and can receive its guidance. But when you speak with restriction, you identify with your personality's focus on limitation and trigger your thoughts to continue along a narrow track.

For example, if your personality resists Not Knowing and is anxious for the security of concrete answers, you may automatically say, "I just don't know what to do. I wish I knew!" Immediately your mind will go to work looking for answers, trying to fill the Not Knowing with knowing. Then you miss the opportunity to expand.

To practice talking about your yearning and Not Knowing in ways that reinforce your openness to unlimited possibilities, take some time to sit and use the following conversational guidelines with a trusted friend. It is important that this person agrees to listen without giving you verbal feedback, advice, or suggestions. The ability to listen and to receive your experience is her or his greatest contribution.

◆

Attunement
Talking About Yearning and Not Knowing

1. Begin by describing your yearning. Open your heart and tell how it feels. If you have visions, emotions, physical feelings, or sensations of energy that come from the yearning, describe them. Your yearning is valuable; treat it as a treasure you are showing your friend.

2. After you speak about your yearning, spend just as much time describing the Not Knowing. Allow the Not Knowing to present itself to you in its strength and openness. Describe it in detail to your friend, and do not try to fill its emptiness. Sitting with its

emptiness may bring you to its spaciousness and beauty. For example, you may say something like, "The Not Knowing is just blank space, empty space." Next you may find yourself saying, "You know, its emptiness really gives me the time I need to avoid rushing into something. I can move more slowly and consciously."

Of course, what you actually say may be quite different, but the important things are these: (a) Let Not Knowing present itself to you on its own terms; (b) Recognize Not Knowing as your ally; (c) Communicate your full experience; (d) Let yourself speak with the assumption that Not Knowing has purpose. You do not have to know what its purpose is right now. You just need to be receptive to Not Knowing— to what is real and trustworthy about it.

◆

40

Setting Your Course

Any path of transformation will bring you to unexpected cross-roads. Practical decisions must be made. In which direction should you go? What action should you take? Whom should you choose as traveling companions? As goals and values change, your old criteria for making choices may seem feeble or irrelevant. If you do not yet see exactly where you are headed, you may feel doubly at a loss. When you are caught in uncertainty and confusion but have decisions to make, how can you make the wisest choices?

The Not Knowing can help. Although the intellect likes to think that information comes from knowing, most of your true information comes directly from Not Knowing. As we just discussed, if you rely solely on knowing, you are limited by the confines of what your personality perceives or has already experienced. For staying on one plane of awareness, the knowing is exceedingly helpful; for expanding into new territory, the Not Knowing is a greater resource.

To make a choice, first sit with the Not Knowing. Spend time with it. Make your peace with it. Allow yourself to notice your impatience or inclination to hurry through Not Knowing because of insecurity or fear. When you are out of touch with true self, you are particularly vulnerable to fear and to the need to grab at things to do to give yourself a sense of comfort or security. The feeling is, "*That* will make me safe. *That* will make me okay. Doing *that* will make me happy." Or, you may have the panicky thought "If I don't find the right thing to do soon, I'm going to be in a lot of trouble!"

Noticing your version of this inner dialogue can be extremely helpful. It gives you unmistakable feedback that you are identifying with limitation. When you catch yourself in that pattern, take a breath and give compassion to that part of your personality that is suffering because it is out of touch with true self. Acknowledge that you are simply experiencing the limited aspect of your humanness in that moment.

You came into physical form to be human
and, from the midst of human limitation,
to open to unlimited being.

In order to complete your life purpose, you must accept being fully human, which includes living in limitation. A response of fear, panic, and looking to externals for the power that actually comes from true self is proof that you are living the limited aspect of humanness well. Do not be afraid of this. The pure longing to complete your life purpose is so strongly inherent in your being that it will continue to pull you onward no matter how thoroughly submerged in the limited you have become.

After you recognize that the sense of urgency comes from your personality and you extend compassion to it, take another deep breath and gently turn to the longing and Not Knowing as your guidance in what to do. This lifts the decision from the hands of the small self that is trying to stay in control and gives it to the greater self, from which a decision of true empowerment can be made.

How can you do this? One way is to become comfortable with the "Yearning and Not Knowing" meditation described at the end of Chapter 38, "Gathering Power," and to then add some steps for offering your choices to Not Knowing. The lengthened meditation is listed below.

◆

Meditation

Yearning, Not Knowing, and Decisions

1. Close your eyes and allow your breath to take you deep into self. Follow a few breaths into your throat area. . . . Follow a few breaths into your heart area. . . . Follow a few breaths into your belly. . . .

2. As you continue to breathe gently and easily into deeper self, allow your yearning to surface. . . . You may feel your yearning passionately or you may barely feel it at all; it makes no difference. It is not the sensation that is important. It is your intent. When your intent is to allow your yearning to surface, it will happen whether you feel it or not. . . .

3. Continue to sense the yearning as it is. . . . Now also sense the Not Knowing, as though you are silently inviting it to present itself, too. . . .

4. Not Knowing may appear as a blank screen, an empty hole, a beautiful light, or as something else. It may even come as nothing at all: no image or feeling or sense of anything. Open to it in whatever way it presents itself. . . .

5. Allow the yearning and Not Knowing to spend time with you together. . . . Breathe gently and easily into the yearning and Not Knowing, allowing yourself to trust their presence. . . .

6. Hand one of your choices to Not Knowing, and say, "What about this possibility?" You are literally giving the energy of that possibility to Not Knowing so it can reflect a higher perspective to you. . . .

7. Allow Not Knowing to reveal the essence of that choice to you. The choice may become vibrant and full of life, it may become duller, faded, or deadened—or something else may happen. . . . Spend a few moments observing the feeling or image that is presented. . . .

   When you have received the message about a possible choice, put that choice aside and hand Not Knowing the next one. You can repeat the process until you have gotten energetic feedback on all the choices you are considering. If you have several choices to present to Not Knowing and become fatigued before you get through them all, simply take a break until you are rested. Then repeat the meditation for the remaining choices.

8. When you are ready to come out of meditation, turn your awareness to your whole body, noticing how it feels from head to toe. . . . Then slowly stretch, and open your eyes.

◆

The feedback from Not Knowing may be in specific images that you immediately understand, or it may be more abstract or subtle. You may have to go entirely by how you feel. With practice you will become more adept at understanding the "language" you share with Not Knowing. You can then consider the information you receive from Not Knowing as you weigh your choices and make your decision.

If each possibility looks or feels wonderful as Not Knowing reflects the energy back to you, consider that perhaps you cannot make a mistake in your choice. In fact, even though you may not be consciously aware of it, any decision you make comes from some important part of yourself that wants expression. As you follow through on a decision, whether it turns out to bring you joy or sorrow, abundance or loss, or a combination of experiences, some aspect of your being wanted to be expressed, or manifested, and you gave it expression by making that choice. Manifesting and interacting with that aspect of self via the situation you created from that choice exposes you to learning that can enable you to grow and move on.

Sometimes it is better to make a decision and see what happens than to be forever afraid of making the wrong choice. The most important thing is simply that you come fully to life while you are here in this world. Any choice you make carries that possibility.

41

Updating the Map

As you accept your human self, become familiar with your emotions, and take counsel from Not Knowing, a new vision may develop that allows you to look more honestly and creatively at your life. You may begin to question the unnecessary judgments and restrictions you have placed on yourself and others over the years. You may want to release outdated patterns of emotion or behavior that are not empowering, but are limitations you adopted for survival at earlier stages of your life. How can you go about doing this?

Transformation occurs more smoothly and deeply when you are able to extend compassion and love to yourself. Think about loving yourself for a moment. For some people, the mere idea of loving themselves is overwhelming; it seems like too big a job. They unconsciously assume that they are so unlovable by nature that any efforts to counteract that reality would be exhausting or would simply fail. They think that they have to conjure up feelings of love, love, love that never stop. What an arduous task!

If you feel that loving yourself is difficult, you can do three things:

------------------------------◆------------------------------

Attunement
Finding Affection for Self

1. Remember the love that you are. When you remember that unlimited love is always vibrant and alive in every cell of your body, it is easier to feel some love for yourself. Love is something that already exists within you, not something you have to create on the spot.

2. Think in terms of simply having some affection for yourself. Affection seems easier, as though it is a scaled-down expression of love. It is tiny love. In your most self-critical moments, you do not have to stretch so far to find a little feeling of affection for yourself, yet the benefit of that affection will be just as great as if you were enthusiastically in love with yourself. Let tiny love—or even tiny affection—be enough.

3. As you catch yourself repeating your old pattern, take a moment to ask, "Where is my affection for self in this situation?" As you continue asking with genuine sincerity, you will find affection. Even if the old pattern is one of self-hatred or self-criticism, which is terribly uncomfortable, it is still possible to find some inner affection for who you are. It may help to imagine that you are stepping back far enough for a greater perspective. Or, imagine that you are seeing with bigger eyes, eyes that can find even the tiniest affection for self, no matter how hidden it may be.

◆

Let's take a moment to examine what it is like to be caught in an outdated pattern—one so deeply ingrained that it feels as though it will never fade. Looking closely, we find the same two elements we discussed earlier: true yearning and Not Knowing. You yearn for a more expanded way of being that expresses your true self, yet you do not know whether the restrictive pattern will ever change or how that change may happen. In short, you are in the split.

Joining you there is the small self who wants to stay in control. The small self wants to leap over the split as soon as possible and will try to do it by taking immediate action to avoid, deny, or dismantle the restrictive pattern. These efforts, based on control, are rarely effective and most often lead to frustration and an increased sense of the discomfort of being caught in the split.

What can you do? Once again, you will be most effective by being present with yourself and honest about how you feel. "Here I am in the split again, and this is uncomfortable." When you no longer try to flee, you can witness the pattern you have been caught in ("I'm still doing this!"), feel the yearning ("I want a new way of being that comes from my true self rather than from old, restrictive conditioning"), and let the Not Knowing be with you ("I don't know how to make this pattern change, but I'm open and committed to it happening").

Being in the split is like sitting
on top of a pyramid;
whether or not you can feel it,
all energies are aligned to give you power.

Because the predominant feelings in the split are often helplessness, fear, and frustration, the power is easily overlooked and misdirected. Yet whether you are conscious or unconscious about what you are doing, the way you direct your intention determines how the power is used. If you resist the split, resistance is what will be amplified, reinforcing the sense of being caught in a struggle. This will not create much opportunity for changing the pattern that originally distressed you. If, however, you compassionately allow yourself to feel the longing for change and the feelings that go with being in the split (discomfort, anticipation, excitement, fear, etc.), the creative energies of both your longing and your willingness to be present with yourself will be empowered. As you also open to Not Knowing, your ability to draw from the unlimited is strengthened, and new possibilities can come to you.

With this kind of receptivity and empowerment, you are open to transformation and are attuning to your greater potential. In time you may need to take specific actions to support your personality in its change. Proceed, knowing that whatever you genuinely want for yourself and are willing to create through the assistance of the unlimited is truly possible.

Your destiny is not preordained by some outside source. It is inside you, created and re-created in every moment by your own unbounded self. It is as fluid and transmutable as you are. If you do not like where you are going or the weight of the baggage you carry, you can make revisions. Again, you do this not by resisting or controlling what you find on your path, but by redirecting your awareness. Unlimited possibilities await you.

42

Getting Free of Self-Judgment

Feeling separate from the love that you are makes you easy prey to self-judgment. Self-judgment is unrelenting; it never strikes just once, but uses your thoughts to attack again and again. Sooner or later these self-rejecting thoughts can invalidate everything about who you are and the path you are on, leaving you disoriented and confused. Heavy with doubt, you drag your feet and wonder why life isn't more rewarding. This is a sign that it is time to make your predator your prey.

As painful and restricting as self-rejecting thoughts can be, they are not all bad. There is an energy at the core of each that you can use to your advantage, no matter how crippling the content of the thought may be. You can view that core energy as hidden nourishment that is yours to claim. When you are caught in self-sabotaging thoughts, these three steps can help you become present and aware enough to use that energy constructively.

◆

Attunement
Facing Self-Judgment

1. Stop for a moment and realize that self-rejecting thoughts are occurring. It will not help you to ignore them or passively accept them. It *will* help you to ac-knowledge their presence.

2. Let yourself feel how uncomfortable it is to have your energy turned against yourself. Notice that not only is it a mental discomfort, but also it feels uncomfortable to your body to be bathed with critical thought.

3. Use the power of your intention: state that you want the energy within the self-rejecting thoughts to bring you a greater experience of true self.

———————————— ◆ ————————————

So there you are, noticing a painfully critical thought, and feeling the emotional and physical discomfort it causes. From the midst of it, you remind yourself of what you want: "Even in this criticism and discomfort, I want this thought to bring me to a greater experience of true self." Or, to be more accurate, say, "I want the *energy* of this thought to bring me to a greater experience of true self." The distinction between the thought and its energy is important. It is not the content of the thought that will bring you to true self, but the energy at the core of it.

> *You want to align yourself with*
> *the power—the core energy—of thought.*

Energy exists at the core of all thoughts, feelings, things, and living creatures. All creation, whether experienced as pleasant or unpleasant, good or bad, limited or unlimited, carries in its essence the unlimited love and creativity of vibrant life force. The content of any thought is always secondary to the life force the thought carries at its core. That is why "negative" thoughts work as well as "positive" ones for opening you to true self, *if you remember to transcend the content and go to the core energy.*

All things spring from Source. Source is unlimited, unconditional love and well-being. Source is all possibility. The more you are immersed in experience of Source, the more you are immersed in unlimited love, all possibility, and absolute well-being, regardless of what is happening in your life and regardless of what you are thinking. What a beautiful irony to find Source even through your self-critical thoughts! This is quite easy to do and is excellent practice. It reminds you that what seems most real and most enduring to the judgmental mind actually carries the least truth and power if you simply shift your awareness to a deeper level.

Judgmental thought can be destructive to your being if you stay at the content level. Believing the content damages your self-image and hurts your personality. On the other hand, resisting or rebelling against judgmental thought can be very depleting. It means you are always fighting a losing battle. Even if you try to defend against the content of self-judgment by countering with turnaround statements such as "No, I'm not bad, I'm good" or "There's nothing wrong with me. I'm really okay," the critical thinking starts up again the moment you stop your defense. Then you must leap into battle again and again and again. It is an exhausting war.

Again, the core energy of every thought has the power to bring you consciously in touch with true self. Yet, the content of most thoughts you entertain during your day lacks that capability. When you no longer engage with the content of your self-rejecting thoughts but go straight to the Source energy within them that will nurture you, you are freeing yourself from being victimized by self-judgment. Self-judgment becomes, like everything else, just another vehicle to reconnect you with Source.

Source is always the healer.

When choosing Source in the midst of self-rejection becomes your habit, something remarkable takes place, a shift that changes your entire relationship with the world: By disengaging from the content of self-limiting thought and choosing to be empowered and carried forward by the Source energy at its core, you transcend limitation and align with unlimitedness. As you become familiar with this pattern, you will find yourself automatically applying this transcendence to other situations in your life as well.

To see how this happens, take a moment to imagine a threatening situation when you are boxed into a corner and cannot get out. You are trapped, feeling that something terrible is happening to you, yet you are helpless to stop it. Notice that feeling. It is quite similar to the feeling created in your body when your thoughts are harshly judgmental of yourself; your body feels the pain of the self-hostility and the distress of not being able to get away from it.

Now imagine that even though you are trapped, you are able to remember the love that you are or to reconnect in some way with your true self. As you do this, you experience a sense of freedom and natural empowerment. Instead of feeling stress and pain, your body relaxes into ease and joy. It is safe to be expansive. You know that your well-being is assured regardless of what is happening externally, and you sense that the core energy of everything in the situation around you is the unlimitedness of Source and carries all possibilities.

By going through this kind of shift—transcending to Source whenever the distress of self-judgment occurs—your body and personality learn transcendence as a new pattern. After enough repetition, the shift will happen automatically and increase in its scope. As you become used to transcending to Source in the midst of the distress of self-judgment, transcendence to Source will also be triggered in other situations that create the same type of distress in your body.

It is wonderful when this shift becomes automatic. It means that you are naturally seeking the unlimited in the midst of limitation. Sometimes this will occur in such subtle ways that you do not consciously notice it. Other times it will be a delightful surprise. As it becomes second nature, you will rejoice at the well-being it brings you.

Part IX
Awakened Personality

---◆---

Loyal Servant to Unlimited Spirit

43

Transformation and Perfection

Living your life as an ongoing process of transformation is a marvelous adventure. In facing the challenges that come your way, you gain inner strength, develop emotional depth and agility, and learn to transcend limitations that may otherwise continue to lock you into patterns of struggle and unhappiness.

Yet, as with everything, there is a need for balance. An over-reliance on transformation can be an addiction, which occurs when people continuously focus on change because they cannot accept themselves as they are. Because the motivation for this kind of transformation is self-rejection, these efforts toward change become a distraction from being with self. Some pitfalls of this pattern are as follows:

1. No matter how much change is made, it is never enough to be fully satisfying.

2. Because the change that has been made was not based on a sense of well-being, it turns out to be disappointingly limited in its scope or does not last.

3. The basic issue of self-rejection is avoided and is never resolved.

Transformation addiction may be directed inward (changing the self) or outward (changing the world) and often carries a tone of life or death urgency. The basic assumption of the inner directed pattern is, "I must change to be okay"; the outer-directed pattern is, "The world (or other people) must change for me to be okay." The inner-directed dialogue may continue to include any of the following statements. Perhaps you recognize some of them. "In order to grow (or heal), I must change."

"In order to get along better with people or to manifest money or to contribute to the world, I must change." "To be able to live with myself, I must become something better than what I already am."

The need to change yourself (or anyone else) to attain a sense of well-being leaves you at a definite disadvantage. It means living with emptiness and insecurity while you try to become whatever you think is better. The effort you expend to create this change can be endless and exhausting.

This does not mean that you should give up on transformation and be stuck with inner patterns and outer circumstances that do not feel right to you. Growth and change are important. It may be helpful, however, to take an honest look at the attitude that motivates your change. If the beliefs about yourself that prompt your change are healthy, the changes you make will support your greater health. If those beliefs are self-sabotaging, your changes, no matter how dramatic, will have limited benefit.

What if the real truth is that you are enough right now, just as you are? What if well-being is your birthright and will come alive for you in an instant if you are willing to let yourself have it? What if all change and transformation, in you and in the world, are options but not necessities?

Understand that from unlimited spirit's perspective, there is nothing wrong with you; you are perfect as you are. You do not have a flaw or a blemish. Even your suffering or the suffering of others is not a sign that anything needs to be fixed. Everything carries perfection as it is.

Although your personality may find this difficult to accept or believe, nothing about you or about the world needs to be changed for well-being to occur.

Vibrant life flows through all things, all beings, and all situations as they are right now. Unlimited well-being already exists everywhere, although it often is not recognized.

If, tomorrow, every person on earth were to open to the experience of profound well-being and feel the sublime delight of the flow of life force, there would instantly and automatically be a shift in the general consensus about what should be done in the world. There would no longer be panic, urgency, or resistance about making change. Instead, there would be the knowing that Source is alive and vibrant everywhere, in the biggest disasters as much as in the most beautiful and awe-inspiring creations of nature. From there, people would make change from pure choice and alignment rather than from urgency and suffering. Their energies would go into creating an environment for all creatures that expresses the great well-being that already exists.

This intent is very different than trying to change things so people can escape suffering. The experience of suffering is real, but that does not mean it carries the greatest truth. Its reality is based in the personality's orientation to limitation and separation. Actions taken to escape suffering reinforce the belief in suffering as a foundational force of existence.

Recognize that when you identify with life at a superficial level, you are focused within the illusion of limitation, which is where suffering is perceived. At that level, your actions may bring change to the forms in which suffering occurs, but suffering will not be eliminated as long as you believe in it.

Well-being is the natural state
of true self and unlimited spirit.

If you want to transform suffering, bring your awareness to the well-being that already *is* at the deepest level. There, free from suffering, you can make choices and changes from a pure sense of inner peace, regardless of the external situation. Your actions will then carry unlimited creative power and will continue to reveal well-being as the most basic reality.

If you feel an urgency about creating change in your life or in the world, you probably do not experience yourself as a vehicle for the sublime delight of life force. You may be focusing on change to compensate for this lack. Creating change becomes a replacement for what you want most deeply but do not have. Yet, because it is more superficial, making change in yourself or others is much less satisfying than having the full experience of Source. When you are in separation from Source, the change you make—in yourself, in someone else, in the world—is never quite enough. There is always more that calls to you with a familiar urgency.

Again, by no means is this a suggestion that you should stop trying to create change. Being passive and ineffective in the world is no solution to missing your connection with Source. However, you may need to face the strength of your longing for the inner peace of deep connection.

There is one way to tell easily and instantly whether you feel separate from Source: the degree to which you feel anxiety in your life is the degree to which you are in separation.

It is important to distinguish between *feeling* separate from Source and *being* separate from Source. There is no such thing as actually being separate, because Source is in every aspect of your self and your world. For our purposes, being in separation simply means losing conscious awareness of the presence of Source, orienting instead to your personality's reality of separation and limitation.

44

Nurturing Your Personality

Because the personality is such a strong part of your experience of self, you need to take good care of it. This includes honoring it by recognizing its needs and giving it a healthy environment, internally and externally. When you consider making changes in your life, the following four steps may be helpful:

Attunement

Creating Changes in Your Life

1. Begin by dropping the idea of changing yourself to become a better person.

2. Assume for the moment that you are okay as you are and that you can have well-being right now without making any internal or external changes.

3. From that clear space ask yourself, "What does my personality need to be its healthiest?"

4. Make a list of the top one to five actions you can take or inner changes you can make that will support your personality in living in good health and well-being.

You may discover that your personality needs more companionship with supportive friends, more love, a change in your work environment, more play and enjoyment, a sense of accomplishment or challenge, a healthier body to live in, more direct self-expression, or greater attention to your emotions, to name just a few possibilities. For example, your personality may ask you specifically to deepen some friendships you already have and let go of others, or perhaps to persevere in finding new friends who suit you better.

Or, because your body is home to your personality, you may need to give more attention and care to your body. Just as you would not want to live in a house that falls apart, you do not want to put your personality into a body that falls apart from lack of care. You may need to choose foods and activities that will nurture and strengthen your body so your personality can live in a clean, strong, supportive physical environment.

Proper emotional care of self is as important as proper eating and exercise. Your personality may tell you that you need a deeper understanding of your emotional responses, perhaps accompanied by some new options to replace old patterns that no longer serve you; or a release of feelings you have been holding back for too long; or greater compassion for yourself; or a good pat on the back to affirm the emotional growth you have already begun.

You may be able to get your emotional needs met through the support of friends whom you trust to live in truth with you, through a good therapist or support group, or through active involvement with your community in a way that has meaning for you. Be sure to find your source for healthy emotional interaction and growth if your personality requests it. You need open, clear, strong emotional circuitry that serves you in the world.

Tending to your personality's needs
is the basic housekeeping required
for a healthy human being.

How much housekeeping is needed? Emotional clearing, proper diet, proper exercise, and healthy rapport with family, friends, and community all give significant nurturing to the personality. Yet even these health-enhancing actions are completely fulfilling only when accompanied by attunement to spirit.

Spirit is the Source from which personality manifests. For balanced living, the vehicle of expression (personality) must be strongly developed, but it must not be mistaken for the greater consciousness that is doing the expressing (spirit). It is unlimited spirit that links us in unity to all things and all beings; personality on its own cannot do this.

Consider the imbalances that occur when either personality or spirit is ignored. Some people who are strongly oriented to personality ignore spirit and draw on its power only as a last resort. Their overreliance on personality keeps them focused in limitation, creating a life of illusion and attachment. On the other hand, some spiritually oriented people tend to recognize only the value of spirit and deny or resist the importance of personality. This disconnection from personality makes it difficult for their expansive experience to be integrated into their issues of daily living.

Personality's highest function is as a vehicle for spirit. A weakened personality is less able to tolerate the brilliant vibration of spirit, while a healthy personality carries it easily. Because your personality is focused in the physical world, whatever consciousness it carries contributes to your everyday view of the world. Supporting the health of your personality increases your capacity for bringing the brilliance of spirit into your life.

As your healthy personality opens to true self, you surrender to the unlimited. In that alignment there is total well-being; nothing exists that is not well-being. Even a situation in your life that may normally cause you intense suffering is removed of all distress when viewed from this state of enlightened well-being. Such a situation becomes infused instead with unlimited love, compassion, and surrender to the sublime beauty of life. Suffering is replaced by the knowing that nothing is essentially wrong and that only perfection exists. Your attachment to anything outside yourself you had hoped would save you from suffering is automatically dropped. You are already saved, for you are one with Source.

The logical mind can have difficulty understanding this concept. From the personality's focus in separation, it may be hard to imagine and believe in a reality that does not include struggle with fear and suffering. Yet that reality does exist, and true self is waiting to show it to you. Be patient and loving with yourself as you learn to perceive it.

45

Where Is Your Support?

Have you found your unshakable source of support yet? Without it, life can be overwhelming and your path can seem impossibly long or rocky. No matter how rough the going, you need to know that you are cared for and guided and that there is a power supporting you that will not let you down.

Ask yourself, "Where is my truest, most reliable support right now?" You may be aware of support from specific people in your life, but go deeper. Where is support that is even more constant and profound than what another person can give you? Where is support that goes beyond the security you can get from money or a satisfying career? Where is support that is continuous, never wavering for a moment? You are looking for support that is undiminished by anything that happens around you, by what other people do, or by what you gain or lose in the world. You are looking for Source.

Where can you find Source? It is the unlimited; it is everywhere. True self is your link to it, so look within. As you allow true self to become more real to you, you find divine support, around you and within you, that is absolutely unthreatened by anything you may think, feel, or experience. You are bathed in the knowing that, in fact, nothing truly exists but the support of Source.

Meditation is one way to align with Source, and because Source can be found everywhere, any type of meditation can take you there. You may want to experiment with using some of your daily activities as meditations. Here is a sampling of three practical and enjoyable possibilities.

◆

Attunement
Feeling the Support of Source

1. Periodically take time to sit quietly and let your breath take you to your inner Source. With each breath, gently think or speak your intention to connect. You may use words such as, "I align with the unwavering support of Source that is always with me." Let yourself feel the supportive presence of Source. If your mind wanders, simply repeat your affirmation of intent. Enjoy the connection.

2. Take a walk or jog and allow the movement of your body and the beauty of nature to bring your awareness to unwavering inner Source. As you move, periodically use a verbal affirmation, such as the one mentioned above, to direct your intention and keep you on purpose.

3. Talk about your inner Source of support with other people. When you are in touch with it, or would like to be, talking about what Source feels like and how you draw on its support can be a form of mediation. If this talk is not done as idle chatter but is used to take

you into the experience, it can make the inner connection more real. Choose to do your sharing with people, perhaps good friends or a spiritual support group, who can understand and who also want that type of deeper experience.

———————————— ◆ ————————————

46

Personality as Ally

One theme that has emerged so far in this book is that the personality habitually overlooks or rejects unlimited spirit. As the inner navigator who knows how to get us through limited reality, personality seems to have little ability to recognize unlimitedness. Instead, it works hard to stay in control of what it knows. When unlimitedness is experienced, personality often interprets it as a disruption. Its automatic reaction, then, is to try to put an end to the disruption so that it may return to what is familiar. In this way personality resists unlimitedness.

Fortunately, there is also another side to this story, a side in which personality longs for unlimitedness. Because personality is the aspect of our being that experiences separation from Source, it is the aspect of our being in which all suffering takes place. Yet, it truly does not like to suffer.

Even if suffering is a long-established, habituated pattern in your life that seems impossible to break, your personality still does not like it. Perhaps you were given the impression in your childhood that you are most "real" when you are suffering, or that you are living in the most righteous way when you are in pain. This can cause your personality to cling to suffering as a self-affirming reality. Still, even underneath that ingrained pattern your personality longs to be free from suffering and to heal.

When you allow unlimitedness into your conscious awareness enough times, your personality begins to recognize that unlimitedness *is* a possibility. As this exposure continues, your personality becomes willing to support your intention to live without limitation rather than resist. Your personality then begins to stretch, opening to the greater reality in spite of old attachments and beliefs in limitation. Such a turning point is most significant.

Look for those times in your life when there is resistance to unlimitedness. You may notice it when your personality says to you, "This is not real. You are a fool to create your life around unlimited thinking or unlimited action. Who do you think you are, anyway? And what makes you think any of this new stuff will work?" In those comments you are hearing your personality's fear and need for control. Recognize the fear and give it a blessing. You do not need to resist it, for it does not help to resist your resistance. You simply need to feel the distress that it causes in you. Feel the pain of separation from Source and the pain of not trusting your true self.

As you recognize this discomfort and get to know it, you can say, "Yes, here it is again." With that acceptance you are open enough to also add, "In the midst of this distress in my personality, I choose to open to unlimited being. I long for it, and I am willing to receive it. I let unlimited love and well-being fill my body. I allow myself to be a conduit for vibrant life force."

This kind of affirmation of your truest intent has tremendous power. Remember that regardless of whether you feel the transformation in that moment, something important happens from that inner statement. Use whatever image or words seem the most natural for you; you have unlimited creativity. The form of your affirmation is important only to capture your intent; your intent is what will activate the transformation.

47

Bridging the Split

We have talked about the split as being the gap that seems to exist between limitation and unlimitedness in our lives. The split can be perceived in many ways, including our difficulty in creating tangible outer conditions or events that reflect our inner expanded awareness. As long as we experience limitation and unlimitedness as separate rather than integrated, the split will continue to seem real.

We have also emphasized the importance of not trying to escape or reject the split and have looked at ways to make use of the power that lies hidden within it. Understand, however, that you are not necessarily destined to stay in the split forever. The steps you take in exploring the split are meant to take you to a bridge where you can complete your crossing. Or, more accurately, those steps are meant to take you into *being* the bridge that brings your inner transcendent experience into outer manifestation in your world.

The bridge can be found, ironically, in the very aspect of your being that creates the split in the first place: your personality. Its experience of separation is what keeps the split in existence. As it accepts unlimitedness into its awareness and belief system, its reality begins to change; it experiences itself as part of the greater whole rather than as separate. As your personality's reality shifts to include this unity, the split narrows and unlimitedness begins to be expressed in your manifestations in the outer world.

The personality takes on a new role
as it finds its true power in being
the loyal servant to unlimited spirit.

You may notice this shift as a lessening of the gap between your personality's daily reality and your occasions of expanded awareness. You no longer have the sense of needing to give up expanded awareness to function in the limited world, nor do you have to give up personality's daily concerns to live with expanded awareness. The two realities become integrated within you, and that integration becomes noticeable in your external manifestations. It is as though there is more room for you to be all of who you are—everywhere!

Because personality is oriented to physical reality and is adept at functioning in limitation, it knows about manifesting in the physical world. Your frustration in the past was, in fact, that most of your manifestations were straight from your personality and were, therefore, too limiting for the part of you that was growing. Your personality can manifest only what it experiences. If it experiences only limitation, that is what it creates in outer form.

When your personality is integrated with unlimited awareness and experiences it as real, it is able to outwardly manifest that unlimitedness. Then you are able to see outer change in your life that reflects the inner transformation you have been carrying. Whatever you have been seeking—whether satisfying work, relationship, or other situation for expressing true self in the world—is created naturally and appropriately.

This is one area in which having a strong and healthy personality pays off. The clearer and more balanced your personality is and the more adept it is at functioning well in the physical world, the more power of unlimited Source it can bring into the forms it creates in your life. It will be a strong vehicle for conveying the flow of vibrant life.

A healthy personality that has opened its consciousness to unlimitedness will also be able to take action in the world and maintain a sense of true self while doing it. Similarly, it will be able to speak or write and consciously express true self through that communication. And one of its great joys will be recognizing the reflection of unlimited spirit in situations that once seemed filled with limitation.

48

Approaching the Bridge

Just before reaching the bridge of integration, there is a gate. Standing in front of the gate can seem almost like torture. You are impatient and want to cross the bridge. You stand on one foot and then on the other, waiting for the gate to open. You can see where you want to be and can even imagine what it would be like to have a life that reflects the unlimited. True self is becoming more real and limitation more unbearable. Still, the gate does not let you pass.

The most empowering thing you can do while you wait at the gate is to be fully present right where you are. It may be tempting to mentally project yourself across to the other side, by either wondering why you aren't already there or convincing yourself that you are. Letting yourself imagine the new reality can help prepare you for creating it in your life, but mentally escaping into the new reality to avoid being where you are is a form of self-rejection and will only delay your progress.

All true change is made
in a state of self-acceptance.

You will open the gate by accepting where you are. As you face the gate, you have tremendous power that you may not even realize. You have the power to accept limitation. This may sound disappointing, and your response may be, "But I don't want to accept limitation! I want to get away from it!" Consider two things. First, notice that the description given in "Bridging the Split" about the fully integrated state included limitation. When you become the bridge, you will still be functioning in a world where limitation exists, but you will not be caught in the limitation. You will be able to carry the limited and unlimited together. You cannot carry what you resist, so you must be without resistance to either. If you are still trying to escape limitation, you are resisting it and are not ready for the integration.

Second, recognize that accepting limitation does not mean you have to be comfortable with it. You can accept yourself and still not always feel comfortable with yourself. You can accept fear and not necessarily be comfortable with situations where you are afraid. So, you can accept limitation and not be entirely comfortable with it. What is significant about acceptance, however, is that as you witness your discomfort, you sense that at your core you are in well-being. Even if your emotions and your nervous system seem to be struggling with the situation, your inner witness is in well-being and you recognize it as the greater power. This distinction is important.

The willingness to carry the paradox
of well-being within distress is the ability
to hold power.

If you are still facing the gate, you are still developing your ability to hold power and to carry it into your life. After you move through the gate, you will definitely need this ability, so it is with compassionate wisdom that your greater self has you stand on this side of the gate until you are ready for it to open.

The best practice for carrying power is to allow yourself to maintain extended periods of true well-being and connection with Source. That is the power that will ultimately be streaming through your being into your life, uniting you with the infinite possibilities you now hold in your heart.

49

Carrying Power

Power comes from consciously being unlimited. You are unlimited already and always have been. Sustained conscious awareness of your unlimitedness is all that is really needed to make a dramatic difference in your life. With that change, you embody true well-being regardless of whether you are in a situation that is comfortable or uncomfortable, "positive" or "negative." Nothing can separate you from Source.

While you stand at the gate gathering power your system is learning to carry greater and greater well-being. As you choose to align with Source in the midst of all thought, all feeling, and all situations, you are teaching your body about the presence of true self.

It may seem strange that your body needs to learn this presence, but it does. Your body's circuitry has been laid out largely according to your personality's experience of limitation. As you become more aligned with true self, and as the well-being of Source begins to fill more of your physical body, your body's pathways of consciousness are repatterned. It is as though the conduits once were meant to hold a smaller reality, and now they must expand to carry unlimited life.

You may imagine that the very tissues of your body are being taught something new. Every cell has programmed within it not only its physical function but also the ability to experience consciousness. Each cell in your body has some experience of the consciousness of the whole organism that you are. As the inner circuitry grows, the cells are, in a sense, reprogrammed with a greater consciousness and, therefore, a greater vitality. The physical tissues are infused with more vibrant well-being and potential for a healthier, extended life.

50

Discharging Excess Energy

It can be uncomfortable to increase well-being in your body! It may take time for the inner adjustments to occur that will establish equilibrium around the increase of vibrancy you carry. If being so highly charged is something you are not used to, your body may feel the impulse to discharge some of the energy. It is all right to do this; after your body has received the increased charge, it will use the full imprint as the model for expanding its energetic circuitry. That imprint will remain and will be used by your body long after you discharge whatever feels to you like excess.

How you release this energy is important and requires your making some conscious choices. Let's explore some possibilities. At the top of the list of appropriate outlets is physical exercise. Of course, it should be exercise that is beneficial to your particular body type and preferably something you enjoy doing. In exercise you are discharging a buildup of vibrant life force through an activity that is also physically strengthening to your body and, therefore, to your personality. It supports your total well-being and directly increases your ability to carry power in the future.

What if you truly do not wish to exercise or you have a physical condition that does not permit it? Life is unlimited; you always have an alternative. Your body simply needs some kind of extra awareness that supports it in its process of becoming vital. Your imagination is a good resource. Imagining is easy and can be done along with or instead of physical exercise. For example, when you feel the buildup of intense vibration and the need for discharge, take five to twenty minutes for the following inner process.

Attunement
Discharging Excess Energy

1. Imagine your body bathed from head to toe in vitality. . . . Your tissues receive this vitality as spiritual nutrient, and your cells glow with life. . . .

2. As your body is energized by this vitality, it intuitively knows how much energy it needs to keep and how much it needs to release. Imagine that your body releases the right amount through the pores of your skin. Like light shining through a porous cloth, this extra vitality illuminates the space around you and is then released into your life. . . .

3. To close, spend at least one minute allowing your body to feel a comfortable sense of well-being and ease. . . .

Feel free to experiment with different images. Sometimes you may find that the energy wants to leave through certain areas of your body, or you may be inclined to breathe the energy out with each exhale.

When excess energy is released, it is not "gotten rid of" because of anything being wrong with it. There is nothing wrong with it; it is vitality from Source. It would not have been within you to begin with if it did not have something of importance to give you. As you release this energy, it knows, by its own intelligence, where to go in your life. It knows how to guide you and what to manifest, without your having to give it any further thought!

Be creative in finding other ways of energetic discharge that work for you. A hot bath may help, or a quiet walk in the woods. Housecleaning, gardening, or even reading the funnies can be good. Phoning a friend who understands your process and giving a "vibrancy report" is an excellent way to feel the energy and discharge it through talking about it.

Recognizing when you need to discharge excess vibration and consciously choosing a self-nurturing way to do it can stop you from falling into a pattern of unconscious behavior that weakens your system rather than strengthens it. When excess energy is not discharged, any discomfort you feel from increased vitality may prompt you quite automatically and unconsciously to numb, distract, or subdue yourself. You may do this by drinking caffeine, over-eating or under-eating, eating sugar, over-exercising or under-exercising, escaping into mental activity, over-focusing on a relationship, using drugs or alcohol, or turning to other types of addictive or potentially self-destructive behavior.

So as you take in new levels of vibrant life, be aware of whether it is at all uncomfortable for you. Take responsibility for creating rituals that allow you to receive vibrant well-being, to direct it, and to release it into your life. This is vibrancy management and is your secret for carrying power.

51

Moving Through the Gate

Your acceptance of limitation and familiarity with well-being open the gate; then your ability to identify with the unlimited will move you through it. You cannot force or control your movement through the gate any more than you could have forced the gate open or could have flung yourself across the split to begin with. Making the shift from identifying with the limitation in your thoughts and experiences to identifying with the unlimited is what propels you forward.

Why is it necessary to accept limitation in order to stop identifying with it? You identify with everything you resist. To stop identifying with limitation, you must stop resisting it. When you do stop identifying with limitation you still experience it, but it becomes just another of life's explorations. It is no longer incorporated into your sense of self, and it no longer keeps you from being and expressing all of who you truly are.

Moving through the gate and becoming the bridge changes your life in tangible ways. For example, if you have been struggling to find work that allows you to relate to the world from your expanded awareness, that work will manifest. If you have been looking for a relationship that supports you in being all of who you truly are, you will find your partner. If you have longed for an outer abundance to reflect the sense of abundance and well-being that has begun to grow within you, you will find that, too. The list of possibilities is endless.

What manifests for you in the world comes directly from your sense of self.

To the degree that you identify with limitation, you carry it in your sense of self. That limitation manifests into your world. As you identify less with limitation, your outer manifestations reflect less limitation. Similarly, as you identify more with unlimitedness, you carry unlimitedness in your sense of self, which is expressed through your outer manifestations. You then live with more situations that recognizably reflect unlimited being and support your expanded awareness.

Understand that identifying with unlimitedness or limitation is not the same as identifying with what is "positive" or "negative." It is the limited aspect of the personality that thinks in terms of "positive" and "negative" and judges everything accordingly. Personality may firmly believe that certain thoughts, emotions, and situations are positive and others negative. To guide you through that reality, personality may tell you that you should think more positive thoughts or relate only to the positive experiences if you want to live in a positive world.

The hidden, self-defeating message in this belief is that anything perceived as negative is potentially dangerous. Therefore, the need to avoid, deny, or resist the negative by continually turning to the positive actually keeps you identified with danger and disempowerment. If you are content to remain at your personality's level of limitation, avoiding negativity may seem appropriate. But if you intend to expand your awareness of yourself, others, and the world beyond the narrow confines of identification with limitation, you will need to recognize that nothing is innately positive or negative.

Positive and negative are simply personality's translation of comfortable and uncomfortable, trusted and not trusted. Yet because Source, the vitality of life and brilliance of all creation, is the core energy of all thoughts, feelings, and situations, how can anything be innately negative? With unlimited love, unlimited possibility, and absolute well-being as the essence of all your experiences, pleasant or unpleasant, where is there true danger?

You can afford to be all embracing.

It can be helpful to notice when something seems pleasant or unpleasant to you, comfortable or uncomfortable, safe or unsafe, life enhancing or depleting. Use that information to make your choices. That is part of honoring your personality's needs and is at times necessary for protecting yourself or supporting your emotional and physical health. Yet, you work against your movement into greater awareness if you reject or resist all thoughts, feelings, and life situations that your personality perceives as negative. It may serve you, sometimes, to look beyond the discomfort and "negativity" and connect with Source, which is at the core of whatever you are experiencing.

◆

Meditation

Moving Through the Gate

1. Breathe gently and easily, allowing each breath to take you just a little deeper into the core of your being, deeper into who you truly are . . .

2. As you breathe deeper into yourself, you breathe into a profound sense of well-being. . . . You do not need to try to create this well-being or do anything to make it stronger. Unlimited well-being is already within you, and your breath gently and easily takes you to it. . . .

3. The gate through which you will be passing is in this well-being. As you move into your true self and into the well-being, you find the gate. . . . As you stand in front of the gate, it opens for you. . . .

4. To move through the gate, draw on Source energy in the midst of all your thoughts, all your emotions, and

all your physical sensations. . . . It is vibrant life and unlimited love that is most real amidst all you experience. . . .

5. If you feel any excess energy in your system, let it be released through the pores of your skin into the world. . . .

6. To close, let your body be bathed with a feeling of comfort and relaxation. . . .

◆

Part X
Planetary Survival

---◆---

Facing Challenge in the World

52

Deepening Your Awareness

Your breath has intelligence; it can guide your awareness to the core of true self the moment you ask it to. You can draw on this intelligence right now. For the next few moments, notice your breathing and imagine that you are allowing each breath to take you into true self. Only a slight change is necessary; you are closer to true self than you think. Let the next breath take you just a little deeper. . . . And the next breath a little deeper still. . . . And the next breath. . . .

When you start your day with a few minutes of presence in true self and return to it periodically as the day progresses, you literally change the quality of your life. You operate from a new inner depth and, therefore, relate to a deeper level of everyone and everything around you. At the end of the day, even though you may have gone through the normal course of events and have had your usual reactions and responses to people, something will be different. The world will have left a new imprint on you, and, whether you noticed it or not, you will have had a new effect on other people.

Living from even a slightly deeper place
within yourself expands your perception
of the world around you and enriches
your interactions with other people.

This does not necessarily mean that you will be calm or happy all the time, that people will do what you want them to do, or that nothing will bother you anymore. It does not even mean that the events in your life will occur any differently. It is the quality of your life that will transform. You will become more fully present, closer to essence awareness and a state of well-being that remains constant regardless of any fluctuations in feelings or circumstances. You will become more centered in truth.

This transformation matters because you are part of a planetary shift in consciousness, a consistent worldwide progression into deeper, more expansive levels of self. The world you experience in ten or twenty years will be very different from the one you experience today. You are part of this world, intimately connected to everyone in it; the greater awareness you develop in your life is your personal contribution to planetary growth.

53

Survival and the One Mind

In spite of the spiritual transformation taking place, thinking about what the world may be like in ten or twenty years can be somewhat disquieting. The current atmosphere of crisis on the planet stems from real and widespread problems relating to environmental imbalance, unresolved wars, starvation, health issues, economic instability, human rights, societal violence, and the dangers of atomic power and weaponry. Clearly the path we are following needs some major repair work if we expect it to take us into a healthy future.

Many people who hold a spiritual focus relate to this crisis with fear and panic. "We must hurry up and evolve or we will not survive!" What an interesting contradiction: belief in the power of spiritual evolution and fear for survival—both in the same thought. But spiritual evolution is a given; there is no need to fear that it will not happen or that it will not happen fast enough.

The human species and the planet will survive and thrive.

Throughout human existence, people have always had reasons to be concerned for their survival. What makes current survival issues particularly significant is that they are no longer limited to individual, personal concerns ("Will my self/family/country survive?"), but now extend to fears and deep caring about the condition of the entire planet. This is logical because we know we now have the power to destroy life on that great a scale. And along with the development of this destructive power have come our first photos of planet Earth taken from space, tangible proof that we are one population sharing one home, undeniably interconnected and interdependent.

The result of the recognition of our united existence and our united vulnerability is that individuals can no longer struggle solely on their own, in an isolated way, with their personal issues of survival. Because it is the survival of the world that is now at stake, it is necessary for all people to become aware of their effect on the planetary whole. And from there it must go a step deeper still.

The group mind, the consciousness shared by all beings on earth, must become apparent and experienced as real.

Let's step back for a moment and review this from the broader perspective. Unlimited love is the essence of our being. It is the building material for all forms of life and all events that occur everywhere on earth. As the Source of all creation and existence, unlimited love is what is most real. It is also what is most enduring: it cannot be destroyed. The forms of its expression can be changed, but the unlimited love and creative intelligence of vibrant life force cannot be harmed. It knows only joy, the joy of being.

Consider that unlimited Source does not fear for its survival. Because it recognizes all occurrences as creative manifestations of its love, it is not afraid of anything. It never forgets that what is most real is the love and vibrant life that is at the core of all experience.

Being fully aware of itself, unlimited Source also notices that the manifestation of itself called "the human personality" believes in fear and lives daily with limitation. Personality longs to evolve beyond the constraints and suffering of its limited reality into the expansive well-being of unlimited life, and this creates a pull on Source to assist. Assistance comes through events that allow personality to grow on its own terms, involving issues that personality recognizes as real.

Personality's most fundamental concern is its survival. Because it experiences itself as more real than unlimited spirit, it fears the loss of itself more than anything. Personality wants to preserve its way of organizing the world around itself, and is very resistant to any drastic change. This means that survival issues get personality's full attention the moment they arise.

With support from the greater consciousness of Source, we have all created the current planetary crisis to assist personality in recognizing the oneness we all share. The most basic level of personality survival now literally depends on the world's people coming together with one mind, one intent, one purpose: to find values and actions that nurture the earth and its residents.

Your greatest personal contribution to the survival—and *thrival*—of the planet can be made through experiencing the connection you share with all beings on the planet. There is nothing you have to do to unite with others, for that union has already occurred; just by existing you are naturally in the One mind. One mind emanates from Source and is the unlimited thought and creativity shared by all beings. What now matters most is directing your conscious awareness to this connection.

Understand that being in One mind does not mean that everyone thinks the same thoughts; it is not a mass joining of the personality's intellect. Nor does it mean that you lose any of your autonomy. You will continue to be the full individual you have always been. One mind is simply an interconnectedness in spirit that transcends personality's experience of separation and limitation.

One mind is the life force intelligence
shared by all beings.

As you become aware of your participation in One mind, you open the door for expansive thought to come into your conscious daily life where it can be put to practical use. You are essentially reaching into a realm in which all possibilities are held in "potential," inviting them to move through you into "real life." Naturally, this broadens the range of information and creative impulse you draw from as you create your life and make your contribution to planetary transformation.

This expansion will come as you regularly witness your union with all beings. You can practice this witnessing through meditations like the one at the end of this chapter or by imagining it from time to time during the day. As your natural place in One mind becomes real to you, your personality will be able to receive and use the unlimited creativity that is shared in unity. This connection will bring a subtle, new power to your thoughts, ideas, and actions.

In One mind, you are sharing
a limitless resource of thought
with all beings on the planet.

One mind is a collective pool of thought, which means that everyone draws from it. This resource is not made up of specific ideas so it is not limited to, or even influenced by, the human intellect. It is pure thought. It is the source of all ideas, yet it is infinitely more than ideas; it is the unlimited.

In other words, One mind is not a network through which everyone exchanges ideas. Getting an idea is not a matter of reaching into this reservoir and pulling out a thought that suits you. Instead, the vibrant energy of unlimited thought always moves through you. It is your brain that translates the energy of pure thought into your personal thoughts, doing so according to your sense of reality. Your ideas, then, arise within your physical identity, but the essence energy of those ideas comes from your connection with all beings and all possibility.

You may know other people whose ideas are similar to yours. There are always groups of people translating the unlimited vibration of thought in similar ways. Yet each idea that is shared by the group still begins in the physical identity of each individual. The idea itself is not any more real than that. What is real—before, during, and after the life of the idea—is the vibrant energy of unlimited thought.

This relates directly to the transition of the planetary consciousness. Remember that over the next ten to twenty years as you move deeper and deeper into self, you will literally be living in a different world. This is not just because the world will have changed, but because you will have connected to self and, therefore, to everyone and everything, at a deeper level.

Your use of thought will be affected by this change. Your contact with the deeper level of self will attune your awareness to a more refined vibration, a different frequency from what you identify with now. It will enable your brain to interpret the energy patterns of pure thought in ways that it cannot presently do. You will translate thought into ideas that, at this moment, seem beyond you because you are not yet consciously connected with true self at such a deep level.

The profound ideas that will contribute to the thrival of the planet will come from a refinement in the translation of unlimited thought into ideas. As you continue your commitment to move deeper into self in your daily life, you assist this process of evolution. The deepening of your conscious connection with true self and One mind will increase your ability to hold awareness at a more refined vibrational frequency. And the energy patterning of your new sense of self will manifest as more expansive thoughts, actions, and life experiences.

Recognize the contribution this allows you to make to the world. Perhaps your way of working for a more harmonious planet includes, or even centers around, political activity or making changes in your lifestyle. Yet even in the midst of your life-enhancing practical action, the most powerful thing you can do is to continue to contact deeper levels of self. This will keep the energetic circuitry open for your actions to have greater effect, and will provide you with the necessary attunement to bring creative, new solutions into the world.

◆

Meditation

The One Mind

1. Let the natural intelligence of your breath align you with who you truly are. Each breath knows exactly where to find your true self and takes you there instantly. . . .

2. As you gently breathe yourself deeper, let imagination show you your connection to the group consciousness, the One mind of all beings on the planet. . . . The One mind has a vibrant pulse of life to it. It carries unlimited love and unlimited thought directly into your being. . . .

3. Notice that this vibrant essence of unlimited love and unlimited thought is greater than the personal you, yet your mind translates it into ideas and perceptions, literally creating your experience of the world. . . .

4. The energy of thought moves through your being and is then released to become unlimited, unformed thought once more. . . . Continue to witness the One mind as it enters you, is translated into your world, then flows on to become the One mind once again. . . .

5. As you continue receiving the One mind, notice the unlimited love it circulates through you. With each breath, allow your body to feel the joy of having this energy of love move directly into your tissues. . . .

6. Imagine that this love radiates through your body and out the pores of your skin, directly into your personal world, the world you live in every day. . . . Unlimited love goes directly into everything in your environment. It goes into the metal of your car, into the material of your home, into the clothes in your closet. . . .

7. Slowly open your eyes and look around. Be aware that this emanation of love and unlimited thought continues as you go about your life. . . . You have witnessed your connection with the One mind. You have allowed it to touch you, to become more real to you, and to come into your conscious life.

◆

54

Transforming Fear

We live in a time when the personality's survival issues are being globally stimulated, and fear about the possible ruin of the planet is at an all-time high. Many genuinely frightened people point to past, present, and future-predicted disasters, caused by humans or by nature, and declare those disasters to be evidence of how close the planet is to destruction.

Fear is beneficial to the extent that it prompts you to take notice of the realities you are living with and motivates you to take constructive action. It can be a healthy wake-up call, releasing enough adrenaline into your system to help you move through old patterns of denial or inaction. But if fear is often overwhelming you and causing you to shut down or to identify with doom, something is amiss. You are caught in a closed circuit of limitation in which fear is working against you rather than for you.

Crisis is meant to be identified,
not identified with.

Remember, you manifest what you carry in your experience of self, especially the issues you identify with or believe to be most real. As you identify with fear and disaster, the energy patterns of that identity emanate into your world and take form, perpetuating the very distress that already overwhelms you.

This does not mean you should resist your fear (or other feelings) or that you should ignore distress in the world to prevent manifesting more of it. You do not manifest everything you feel or observe or respond to, but rather only what you carry in your identity. In fact, refusing to allow certain feelings or look at specific issues will not keep you from identifying with them; it will just keep you out of touch with what you are carrying.

So what can you do when you hear about disasters, present or predicted, from people who are in a state of fear or panic themselves? These four steps may help you make constructive use of what can be an overwhelming cultural input of frightening information.

---◆---

Attunement
Responding to People's Fear

Step 1: Be aware of the fear those people are projecting. Then notice where that fear resonates in yourself. Survival fears may center around your basic human needs such as having enough money or a loving relationship. Or, you may be afraid for your physical survival or for the survival of the whole planet. Notice the kind of fear you are feeling, then acknowledge it as your own.

Step 2: Sit for a few moments and support yourself in accepting your fear. Most people do not do this. They will try to skip over the fear and go directly into action, complaint, or denial because underneath the fear they feel helpless and alone.

There is nothing wrong with your fear. It does not weaken you or make you a less spiritual person, nor does it necessarily make you less effective in the world. In fact, fear carries strong energy that can be consciously directed into constructive thought and action. You can take advantage of this hidden power by giving yourself time to notice the fear. As long as it is there, go ahead and feel it. Let it have its expression and be real. "So this is what it feels like to be afraid for my survival." Allow the fear to fully reveal itself.

Step 3: Drop into a deeper level of self that is just beyond fear. The fear may still be with you, but it is not all that exists. Along with the fear is something greater, a greater aspect of yourself that carries the truth of unlimited love and well-being. Your breath can take you there instantly. Let each of your next ten breaths breathe you deeper into true self, gently and easily.

Step 4: As your breath continues to take you deeper into self, allow yourself to witness your connection with the planetary whole. Let your imagination show this to you. It may come to you as an image of being joined with everyone else on the planet, or you may simply feel or sense the unity.

If you need to begin imagining this on a smaller, more personal scale, picture yourself being in One mind with your neighborhood or with your friends. Perhaps you will find it easier to join with your town or your state or your country. The size of the group does not matter. Witnessing your connection in One mind with a small group is just as effective as witnessing it with the entire planet. One mind is One mind; no matter how you picture it, you are witnessing the connection you have with the entire world.

Sit for a few moments in the experience of One mind. It connects you with other people in spirit, in love, in unlimited thought. Enjoy the aliveness and vitality of that connection.

◆

55

Attachment, Suffering, and Disaster

Many situations considered disasters by human beings are quite natural and necessary occurrences in the broader spectrum of nature. Floods, droughts, earthquakes, volcanic eruptions, fires, hurricanes, tornadoes, and other cataclysmic events have always occurred as the pulse and breath of our planet's evolution. Similarly, through violence, ecological blunders, and economic and political crises, humanity exhibits its extremes in its own struggles to evolve.

The higher collective consciousness, of which we are each a part, knows how important survival issues are for bringing our separate identities into awareness of the One mind, and thus "disasters" will continue to be a part of human life for some time.

The most frightening thing about disaster is that it threatens our attachments. We tend to be attached to material things, to people, to being free of pain, to having certain feelings, to remaining alive, and to an array of other conditions. Of course, it isn't wrong to want these things. It is quite understandable that our personality would seek safety, comfort, and companionship; personality has a desire to be healthy and vital in every way possible. Yet desire and attachment are not always the same thing. If our sense of well-being is threatened when our desires are not fulfilled, or when we fear they may not be fulfilled, it is attachment.

> *Attachment is anything the personality*
> *mistakes for true well-being.*

Let's look at the most basic attachment: survival. Survival instinct gives you the desire to remain present and active in physical form. Attachment to staying alive, however, also includes the underlying belief that you will suffer in some way if you die. The aspect of personality that believes that its well-being depends on its physical existence is panicked at the thought of dying. To the degree you fear that death means losing something vital to your *true* existence and *true* well-being, you will be attached to survival in the physical realm.

At the root of every attachment is a belief in limitation. If you know in every fiber of your being that unlimited essence is what is most real, the thought of dying will not bring you panic, pain, or suffering. You may still desire to stay physically alive, but your desire will come from a *true* desire rather than from mere attachment.

It can be difficult to recognize attachment in a relationship because love and attachment can be entwined. You may be tempted to say, "Well, it's okay to rely on other people for my sense of well-being because they are more than material objects. Material things like money, cars, and houses have less spiritual value, but people are really important." At one level of the personality, that is so. At another level, a dependency is a dependency, and you cannot "upgrade" by choosing a loftier one. It is your reliance on a person, a place, or an experience to replace your greater truth that makes it an attachment.

When you open to true self you will eventually encounter an experience of loss related to each of your attachments. Initially, as you allow the light of true self to fill your life, the unlimited joy and pleasure of Source becomes more real to you. In its expansiveness, the light radiates into your fears, loosening your personality's grip on attachments. Sometimes the process of releasing your hold on limitation will be easy, giving you a deep sense of relief. Other times it will be more arduous and painful, stimulating the kind of fear and grief you had hoped all your life to avoid. Sooner or later in your reach toward Source, each attachment will be challenged and must be relinquished.

Some people move through this process with outer dramas. They lose their homes in fires; they lose loved ones in accidents; they lose their jobs during a recession. They may do this sequentially, facing a new loss every few years or so, or they may do it all at once, losing everything in one disaster.

Other people go through the process of releasing their attachments internally, without manifesting much of an observable outer loss. For example, discord may surface in their marriages, prompting a long, painful process of introspection.

They may learn to emotionally let go of their mates and to release their attachment to relationship as their primary source of well-being. The result may be that they work out their problems and do not lose their marriages. Or, shake-ups at work may force them to stop relying on their jobs as their source of personal identity, but they may not end up losing their jobs.

Attachments distract personality from truth, directing our awareness away from recognition of our unlimited being. A belief that our survival depends on having money, a home, a good car, nice clothes, or even good physical health reinforces the illusion that these limited things are the source of our existence and well-being.

Consider that your survival
may depend solely on your alignment
with unlimited spirit.

The vital life force of unlimited being, streaming through your body and your energy system, is what gives you physical life and consciousness. It is also the unlimited Source that carries the true joy and pleasure of being alive. No material thing or other physical being can give you the supreme happiness of conscious surrender to unlimited life force as it carries you forward in the world. If you are out of touch with Source, fulfillment of your attachments will be a weak and temporary compensation, not a satisfying replacement.

There is no reason to feel bad about yourself for your attachment to externals. That's just part of your personality's way of relating to the physical world. Yet it can be helpful to witness your attachments and recognize them honestly for what they are: attempts to compensate for feeling separate from Source. Doing this can make you uneasy because it brings your focus to the inner disconnection with which you have been living, and that is by nature uncomfortable. Still, it is helpful to witness this disconnection compassionately, staying with your-self and not turning away in spite of the discomfort or disorien-tation you may feel.

You long to be whole. You long to know the unlimited love and joy that is your true nature. If you feel separate and afraid—even secretly disappointed in life—your disconnection from Source is important to recognize because it is essentially the cause of all your suffering.

All suffering is separation from Source.

Let's look at what this means in terms of your fears about survival. If one or more of your primary survival fears were to manifest you would probably call it a disaster or a catastrophe. Losing your house and all your belongings in a flood may be one such event, and perhaps you would fear it because of the suffering you would feel. Yet losing your home does not cause suffering; losing your home and not being aware of unlimited Source streaming though your being causes the suffering.

Many people fear having a debilitating or terminal disease. Such an illness can certainly create physical and emotional pain, exhaustion, and ongoing distress. Yet, as uncomfortable as the illness may be, it is not the cause of suffering; illness without conscious experience of unlimited Source is the cause of suffering.

Even pain is not necessarily suffering. Pain is simply pain —an intense sensation that is filtered through our conscious-ness, where it is interpreted according to our reality. It is inter-preted as suffering only when it is not received with conscious awareness of a well-being that goes deeper than any sensation: the well-being of Source.

In fact, living in any way without noticing the vibrant flow of Source through your being causes suffering. You can have an abundance of money, a beautiful home, excellent health, lov-ing family and friends, and all the other "right" things and still suffer quietly and endlessly. Even though all your attachments are fulfilled, you are still suffering through a disaster.

All people affect, and are affected by, each other through their participation in the collective consciousness. Because of this inherent connection, groups of people will act out the various survival issues of the whole planet to help bring growth and alignment to everyone on it. So, at different times and places, people will display, through their personal lives, the planet's collective suffering of disconnection from Source. This will often be done through their participation in disasters.

You may witness these disasters because you live nearby or know the people involved. Or you may witness them on television or in the newspaper. As a witness, you are in a sacred position. You are watching the display of an issue that connects you to those people, no matter how far away they are—physically or culturally. You are watching a situation that unfolds, in part, for your own growth as well as for the contribution you can make back to the whole by your response.

When you see other people suffer, you witness their disconnection from Source. If seeing their suffering hurts you or causes you to criticize or judge them, it is because they reflect the pain of your own disconnection. This situation can be valuable if you let compassion open your heart to yourself and to your feelings. Then let compassion join you to the others who share your suffering and are displaying it for you.

56

From Crisis to Compassion

Responding to a disaster from compassion rather than from crisis can be a tall order. Facing our disconnection from Source can seem overwhelmingly frightening. In fact, many people feel so threatened by their inner disconnection that they stay completely unconscious of it and don't let themselves feel it or deal with it at all. The result is that they automatically react to disasters, theirs or others', with instant fear or blame.

For most people, denial of the pain of disconnection is so strong that daily living is focused on attachments—external things, people, or specific situations—in an attempt to find happiness and security that would otherwise come from Source. This is a type of addiction. Ironically, the suffering from disconnection can be pushed so far into the unconscious that it takes the impact of a disaster to break through.

Disaster often causes the loss of one or more primary external attachments. It can jar people out of their pattern of addiction and force them to reevaluate their lives. For example, losing your home can force you to look at how deeply you relied on your possessions for a sense of identity and security. You may then have the motivation to look within to find your true identity, recognizing that the external world reflects that identity for you but does not create it. Similarly, losing your job or your life savings can force you to face questions about where you believe your true source of support exists and how fully you are able to trust it and rely on it.

Any event involving loss can trigger underlying panic and pain that comes from your personality's persistent attempts to maintain control in a world that is, in actuality, beyond its control. To "recover" you may need to surrender to an inner well-being that enriches your life regardless of external circumstances and then carefully re-create your life based on that surrender.

Losing loved ones, or even losing a relationship with them, can be the most trying disaster. All healing from this loss must be done with compassion and patience for self. Most close relationships are a combination of true, open-hearted love and the personality's projected need. Projected need—wanting the outer relationship to fill the empty disconnectedness within self—is where attachment has its hold. With loss of relationship it becomes necessary to face this inner emptiness and discover more of the fullness of your own being.

Some people who experience disaster are able to use it as a catalyst for freeing themselves of the attachment that is shaken loose. They let their lives be forever changed by that break in addiction. Seeing with a new focus, they learn to make choices that come from deeper truth. Others return to the addiction as soon as the outer crisis is over.

Whether you directly experience disaster or witness it elsewhere, you always have the opportunity to let the situation touch you and bring profound change into your life. You can allow the outer disaster to be a mirror, reflecting your inner disaster of living in disconnection from Source. Feel whatever emotions are present. Open to your suffering without turning away from it; from there you have the power to make new choices and to create new possibilities.

Witnessing the suffering of others from a catastrophic occurrence can be traumatic, even when the event is witnessed only through the media. Because of their difficulty in coping with the trauma, witnesses often try to find order in the situation by making rationalizations or by passing judgment on the people who are the "victims" of the disaster. In an attempt to leap past their discomfort at being separated from Source, witnesses may react to the situation by saying such things as, "Those people must have done something to deserve (or create) this." "Their way of living has been so out of balance that nature (or God) is teaching them a lesson." "It is their bad luck (or bad karma) that has made this happen to them." "Those people really don't feel things the same way we do."

The list of possible judgments goes on endlessly and serves as a way of distancing ourselves from suffering. This is done automatically, and usually unconsciously, to avoid having the suffering of others remind us of our own distressing separation. Passing judgment is a very human thing to do, and it is not "wrong"; but it also is not helpful. It prevents us from going deeper into self where reconnection with Source can take place.

If you notice yourself rationalizing, judging, or dismissing someone else's suffering, you can do something to gently nudge yourself out of this automatic, limited reaction.

Attunement

Finding Compassion in a Crisis

1. Take a deep breath and give yourself a few quiet moments.

2. Recognize your judgment as a sign that you need to have compassion for your own deep, perhaps hidden, suffering.

3. Let yourself experience the discomfort, to whatever degree it may be there, of feeling out of connection with Source. Feel the distress of missing it now. You may also feel the pain of having missed it at certain times in the past.

4. Let yourself feel how much you long for conscious experience of your unlimited spirit, how much you long to feel the vitality and love of unlimited Source streaming through your being, bringing you joy and genuine well-being.

5. Gently take five to ten more breaths, imagining that each breath takes you a little deeper into your true self.

6. From that deeper place, allow the unlimited love that is the essence of your being to begin to flow through you and bring comfort and connection.

57

Allowing Integration

Regardless of how you go through the process of loosening your grip on attachments and no matter how difficult it may be, letting go and turning your awareness toward Source opens you to the greater light of unlimited being. The inner emptiness you tried to fill with attachments eventually becomes spacious rather than vacant. It becomes an opening through which vibrant well-being can enter your life.

As you begin to live with new fulfillment, you may encounter some unexpected feelings of grief. Even though you may have a more expansive sense of self and feel a deeper love and joy, your personality may still need to grieve the loss of the attachments it had carried for so long. This is part of its adjustment to the new reality you are creating for yourself. So be aware that at times when you come into a profound expansiveness of being, there can also be a sense of loss. This feeling is quite natural. Feel the joy and feel the grief, too. Accept the full range of who you are in those moments.

Understand also that your transformation may take you back and forth between seemingly opposite inner realities. For a while you may live in the expansiveness of your being, genuinely feeling less attached to externals. You may relate to work, to people, and to material things from a place of deeper, unshakable connection with true self. Then, a few moments or days or weeks later, you may suddenly feel caught up in your old attachments again, as though you are not free of them after all. This process of cycling through one awareness to the other is part of the integration of newly learned experience. At such times have patience, stay present with yourself, and continue allowing your breath to return you to Source.

◆

Attunement

Witnessing Your Attachments

When facing your attachments, your first act of compassion for yourself is to allow the attachments to be there. Let the attachments be okay. You do not have to get over them. It is too much to expect yourself to notice attachments *and* get over them at the same time; your personality will resist that kind of pressure. You can, however, notice your attachments and give yourself permission to have them. That is compassionate witnessing.

Notice your attachments as they surface, and jot them down. This week you could probably make a list of ten or more things you are attached to. You may want to keep it on the refrigerator, like a shopping list, where it will be accessible. Give the list two columns, and use it in the following way:

1. Each time you notice an attachment, write it down in the first column. There's no need to put in much description or explanation. Just name the attachment. For example you might write,
   "Today I was attached to:
   ◆ Money
   ◆ My child
   ◆ Getting my way at work
   ◆ Finding a relationship
   ◆ Eating sweets"

2. After you identify each attachment, use the second column to write what you were hoping to get from it. For "money" you may put "sense of safety" or "security." For "my child" you may have hoped for "feeling

like I am a complete person." "Relationship" may have been meant to give you "affirmation that I am worthy of love and good things." Eating sweets may have been for "feeling comforted."

Allow yourself to list your attachments with acceptance. You are ready to look at them, which is the first step in releasing them. There's no need to be over your attachments by the end of the week. You just need to explore them. Be honest and forthright with yourself. You are giving yourself an important gift: the awareness of what binds you to this world and becomes your substitute for Source.

◆

Part XI
You Are the Earth

---◆---

Living the One Body

58

Inner and Outer Realities

Our culture has traditionally maintained a strong division between inner experience and outer reality. In this separation, personality has functioned under the assumption that our inner reality is only minimally related to outer reality. Primarily, we have believed that outer reality acts on us and that we respond. For example, we have taken for granted that our feelings are affected, or even caused, by outer occurrences, such as other people's words and actions or events that happen around us. We also have known that our thinking is influenced by what we read, what people tell us, and what we witness occurring.

We have experienced life this way through our personality. Yet, just beyond personality's awareness, a more intimate, reciprocal relationship between our inner self and outer reality has been flourishing. To see it, let's take another look at manifestation.

Your life manifests from your complete sense of self. Whatever you hold in your sense of self—consciously or unconsciously—energetically emanates into the world, creating everything in your life and affecting your responses to it. This means that the inner you projects itself into the world, and then interacts with its own projection. Essentially, you have been meeting manifestations of yourself every day.

This dynamic of manifestation has been going on forever, yet the cultural viewpoint has been that our inner experience does not directly affect our outer reality. There has been acknowledgment that outer reality affects inner reality and that inner experience affects personal interpretation of outer reality. For the most part, however, there has been steadfast insistence that inner reality by itself does not influence what occurs externally. Rather, it has been assumed that outer reality can only be affected by our personal actions or by some other outer influence. The bottom line consistently has been a belief in two separate realities, rather than in a united one.

This separation of inner and outer realities has been valuable in supporting humanity's exploration of limitation. But now that the culture's consciousness is ready to go beyond the confines of life based on separation, something new is happening. The barrier of belief that has been keeping inner and outer realities separate is dissolving.

> *Much of the distress you see in the world*
> *comes from people living*
> *as though everyone and everything*
> *they affect is not them.*

People are willing to put up with all kinds of destruction as long as they believe it is not happening to them personally. This applies to your own life, too. For example, you may believe that the earth's resources are being depleted. Although this issue may deeply concern you, you probably do not feel the depletion occurring the same way you would feel, say, your foot being scratched and scraped. Yet the two occurrences are literally the same thing, and without the belief in separation you would feel them as such. To the degree that you are not fully aware that everything you do in your outer life is something you do to yourself, you contribute to the cultural belief in separation.

Again, now that the culture's consciousness is ready for change, the mass belief in separation is shifting. In a sense, the energetics of consciousness responsible for maintaining the clear division between inner and outer realities is losing its integrity. The old pattern can no longer be maintained. As the pattern transforms, the inner and outer realities begin to blend in humanity's awareness. It is as though these two realities, once separate, have now begun to flicker back and forth with each other. This will continue at increasing speed until there is no longer separation but a merging, a unity. Our awareness will be changed. What we once thought existed only in outer reality will be recognized within us, too. And all that originates within us will be evident everywhere.

This is joyous news. It means that individually and collectively the culture can no longer hold separation in place. It can no longer deplete the earth without people feeling the sensation in their own bodies and emotions. You may already be feeling some of this sensation. If you have a love for the earth and feel pain for what is happening to it, you are in the awakening. It may be uncomfortable, but rejoice in your sensitivity. You are making an important connection.

As the inner and outer realities continue to merge, there is bound to be tremendous disorientation in people's lives across the planet. One place where this particularly shows up is in economics. In most cultures, use of money has been based on the belief in separation between inner and outer. People have thought of money as something separate and manipulatable, unrelated to who they are or who they experience themselves to be. To the degree that this has been true for a culture, that culture's economy is shaken as the field of consciousness that has held the separation in place transforms. The economy becomes unpredictable as the consciousness it reflects moves into a new way of being. No economy (or the world economy as a whole) is likely to stabilize until the cultural consciousness it reflects has stabilized in the new pattern of belief.

Personality judges such economic changes as good or bad. It makes these judgments automatically and arbitrarily, based entirely on how comfortable or uncomfortable the situation is and on how much the change threatens personality's attachments. If the economy takes a turn that causes distress, it is seen as bad. If it is a severe turn or an uncomfortable one that stays for a long time, people's feelings of doom and personality's fears about survival are activated.

Personality's reactions are to be respected for they reflect a reality that is valid on one level of awareness. Yet, we may also want to turn to true self and its unwavering perception of perfection, and take the opportunity to offer its unlimitedness to personality's limitation.

59

The World Catches Up with You

Allow yourself to observe the shift in your life as the separation between inner and outer realities weakens and dissolves. You may notice that it seems to be getting more difficult for you to close off from the world and the people in it. Perhaps you are more easily touched and affected by what you observe in the world. At times you may feel as though all the pain and grief in the world are closing in on you, and you are helpless in the midst of it. It becomes harder for your mind to keep telling you, "That is happening to other people. It doesn't have anything to do with me." Instead, you start thinking, "I never noticed before how bad things really are for so many people. It has never been this bad before, has it?"

The truth is that it has been this "bad," in one way or another, for much of humanity's existence, but you are no longer able to keep yourself so separate from it. Now that you can no longer hold the belief in separation so strongly in place, you are more immersed in the world and more vulnerable to directly experiencing all that is manifested.

*The world is becoming
more personal to you.*

What has always been you externally is becoming more
real to you at an internal, personal level. Increasingly, you may
feel that you cannot get away from what is happening in the
world. It is an accurate feeling; you cannot distance yourself
from the external world because all of it springs from within
you in some way.

This means you cannot make lasting change in the world by
working exclusively to make the change "out there." Because
outer reality springs from your conscious and unconscious
experience of self, it forms itself to reflect you. If you want to
live in a world that is greatly changed from what you now see,
view the world as a reflection of what you carry within. Let the
outer world take you back to its source of creation, your inner
self. That is the place to begin the transformation.

Many people try to hold the outer world out. They see
what is "wrong" out there and try hard to fix it. But all the
while they keep their faces turned from themselves. The world
cannot be fixed in that way. In fact, the world cannot be fixed
at all. Rather, as you let the world back into your heart, back
into your being, it will graciously consent to transformation.

60

Healing the World

You may already be working on this transformation in your
own way. Opening to yourself is the key. When you allow
your deep personal issues of distress and even emotional or
physical abuse to surface in your life, to be consciously felt

and recognized, and to be shared with people who can be understanding and supportive, you are healing the world. You are essentially bringing to awareness the experiences of self you have been unconsciously emanating into the world. Just as the energy of those inner conflicts has been repeating the experience of distress or abuse within your system all this time, it has been contributing to the manifestation of abuse and destruction in the world. As you bring healing to yourself, you are offering healing to the world.

It may be uncomfortable to hear that issues you have been carrying internally, and probably unconsciously, have been "contributing to the manifestation of abuse and destruction in the world." If so, take a deep breath and let yourself be aware that this does not mean there is anything wrong with you. It also does not mean that you are necessarily responsible for anyone else's suffering, violence, or misdirected actions. It simply means that the inner reality you have been carrying has contributed to the cultural and planetary consciousness that has manifested those things.

You are part of the creation of everything
that exists in the world.

It is important to recognize this great influence your inner reality has on the outer world. When you turn away from it, insisting that what happens "out there" is caused "out there," you keep yourself disconnected from your greatest power for creating change: yourself. Nothing can manifest in your outer reality that does not reflect some part of you. As you own your connection to what is manifested, you reconnect with yourself at a level where you can make meaningful change both internally and externally.

Let's look at an example. We have already discussed how your personality fears its own destruction because it does not recognize as real the unwavering support and unlimited life that exists in pure spirit. So, as part of your experience of self, you are carrying beliefs and fears that you can be destroyed. The energy patterns of those beliefs and fears about your destruction emanate into the world where they manifest "out there" in situations that seem to occur independently of you. The possibility of the planet's destruction is a manifestation of this personal issue on a grand scale.

There are innumerable actions you can take to try to prevent the planet's destruction. You can try to change other people's behavior as well as your own. You can try to change people's priorities and ways of looking at how their actions affect the world. Noticeable progress can be made from these efforts, but unless the inner issue also changes, the outer progress will be met with significant setbacks. As long as the inner issue of your own destruction is active, the outer issue of destruction will continue to be expressed in the world.

Facing this outer issue as a reflection of an inner issue provides the opportunity to make peace in the most powerful place first: within yourself. As your personality speaks to you about its vulnerability and fear, showing you the full range of emotion, belief, and personal history that has been causing its distress, you can compassionately accept the existence of its reality. If you do not want to be limited to that reality, within yourself and in the world, you can also choose to allow unlimitedness to come into the experience.

To make that choice, remember the love that you are and the love that exists in all things and all beings. Let yourself surrender to unwavering support that is always with you. Let yourself open to the vibrant flow of life force that is unthreatened and undiminished by any thoughts, feelings, or events. In doing this you will be bringing unlimitedness (the sense of unlimited life, love, and support) alongside limitation (personality's fears and beliefs in its destructibility).

By repeatedly bringing unlimitedness into your inner experience of what is manifested in the world, you will begin to relate more strongly to the forces of indestructibility rather than destructibility. In time your thoughts, feelings, and actions will reflect a greater vision. To support yourself in this transformation, you might follow your favorite suggestions in this book for aligning with true self and unlimited Source. Or, you might rely on prayer or regular meditation, or create your own rituals of empowerment. Find your own ways to call on the unlimited and allow it to become real to you.

Remember that unlimitedness carries greater essential truth than does limitation—and when you carry both in your awareness, the former will affect the latter. As the alignment you hold with unlimitedness begins to teach and repattern your personality's limitation, your experience of self will become more expansive. The energy patterns your consciousness emanates into the world will reflect that new expansiveness and will be your contribution to the collective consciousness.

The collective consciousness manifests world events and situations. And because you are part of the collective consciousness, your expanded awareness will contribute to the creation of tangible global conditions that reflect unlimited love and well-being. Others who are taking practical action to create these conditions will also be supported by your energy.

With this in mind, let's review the main steps for using the power of inner connection to deal with world issues that distress you.

◆

Attunement
Responding to Distress in the World

1. Let any issue that bothers you about the world bring your awareness to the place within you where that issue also lives.

2. Let yourself explore that inner issue as it relates to your personal life, feeling all the feelings, observing the belief patterns associated with it, and sharing your heartfelt experience with trusted support people.

3. As you accept the existence of the inner limitation, find your way to let unlimitedness be real to you, too.

4. Notice your new focus on unlimitedness bringing greater well-being into your life and expanding your perceptions of yourself, others, and the world.

5. Take the outer action toward creating a healthier world that feels genuinely right to you, and remember your inner alignment as you take that action.

◆

61

Sharing Consciousness with the Earth

It's true what they say: the earth *is* your mother. This image is not just poetic. It is true at an essence level. The vibrational pattern of your body is precisely the same as the vibrational pattern of the earth, which means that you and the earth share consciousness. The earth affects you, and you affect it.

Not only do you take in energy directly from the earth, but it takes in energy from you. Whatever is going on in your body is energetically projected outward, and the earth receives it. Because personality lives in your body, your issues about abuse and beliefs about your destructibility are projected out to the earth, contributing to its vulnerability to these same experiences of abuse and destruction.

You cannot stop the natural emanation of your energy patterns to the earth any more than you can keep air from leaving your lungs as you exhale. It will not help to try to control the process by thinking, "I'm not going to project any negativity or destruction into the world." Such resistance to yourself will only create more energy of war and struggle, which will also emanate outward.

Instead, accept the connection you have with the earth and take care of yourself and the earth together. You can begin the process by becoming conscious of your inner issues. Accept that the energy of those issues connects you to the outer world in every moment. Face whatever experiences you still carry that, at some point in your past, seemed threatening to your emotional or physical survival. You may discover forgotten instances of abandonment, neglect, or abuse. Open your heart to yourself as you explore, and get support from other people if you need it. Don't give up on yourself; as you heal yourself you are healing the earth. And because your healing and the earth's healing are one and the same, whenever you want greater healing for the earth, go deeper into the places within yourself that need healing. Your work is there.

Finding inner healing may include accepting feelings of fear or anguish you have avoided all your life. It may also require learning to receive love you never thought you deserved, or to forgive where you never thought forgiveness was possible. As you surrender to your healing, you come to a depth of connection with who you truly are that reminds you that the greatest truth is, and always has been, unwavering perfection. You have the opportunity to embody this truth as you open your heart in compassion to your personality's limitation and suffering and open your mind to your deep memory of unlimited being.

From unlimited spirit's perspective,
perfection is all that has ever existed, and
it is all that exists now.

Our journey Home is our movement into full awareness of this perfection. As we attune our inner hearing to the whispers of higher guidance and true self, we move forward on a path of grand exploration. By giving love to ourselves and each other along the way, we generate the light to reveal each step before us. There is risk, and there is vibrant possibility. With the new reality beckoning, we know only one thing for sure: We will never be the same again.

Epilogue

There is no ending to this book. The journey Home continues in each of our lives. To me, what is most noticeably missing in these pages is your individual story. Some of the chapters may reflect your experience, but the details of your story have a life of their own and may need to be shared directly. You are a traveler in consciousness. Your story of transformation can be a gift to other travelers who long to know that they are not alone.

I am compiling a new book of *Coming Home* stories. It will be a collection of personal accounts of the transition into expanded living. If you have had a life-changing experience of spiritual awakening, I invite you to share it. For example, has unlimited love become real to you? Have you been transformed by opening to true self or higher guidance? Have principles in this book been powerful in your life?

I welcome your contribution as a personal story (up to twelve hundred words), poem, or description of a special dream. Please send it to me, typed, at P.O. Box 1932, Sebastopol, CA 95473. Include your name, address, and phone number so I can confirm your permission to publish your experience.

In the spirit of this sharing, I offer you a dream I particularly cherish. It came at a time when I needed to see deeper into my true self and also to have patience and acceptance for where I was in my life.

◆

My Dream

I stood at water's edge of a large pond. The ground around my feet was covered with a living carpet of little creatures I had never seen before. Full of life and quite beautiful, they were two to three inches long and appeared to be a cross between crustacean and insect. With sturdy protective shells and many legs, they were both strong and delicate. I was at ease in their midst. Their territory extended about four feet up the shore behind me and as far around the pond as I could see. Peering into the pond, I also saw them on the sandy bottom, which sloped downward into watery darkness.

Oblivious to my presence, the creatures busied themselves with movement and with communication that came from sound I could not hear. They were obviously intelligent and organized, flawlessly displaying a system of cooperation I could not quite comprehend. I wondered at their existence.

To me the creatures were unfamiliar, intriguing, and even beautiful; yet I had no feeling for them. It occurred to me that they were more vulnerable in that moment than they knew. If I had wanted to, I could have easily stepped on them. This would have caused them pain and even death; yet because I was so much bigger than they were, they did not recognize my presence and would never have understood what had caused their suffering. It was strange to feel so disconnected from these creatures and yet have so much power over them.

After a few moments, I looked across to the far side of the pond and noticed a beautiful woman standing quietly on a diving board. She was huge, much taller than myself or anyone I'd ever known, and her dress was long and flowing. There was something about this woman that looked a little like me, but she was so much more. She was a goddess.

The woman took a few steps forward to the end of the board, where she effortlessly leapt upward to begin a dive. As she rose, her arms swept over her head in perfect form. She reached the peak of her dive, and I expected her to arch downward and slip gracefully into the water. Instead, she burst. She physically burst. And where she had been just a moment before, the air was filled with the little creatures, raining into the pond.

I was awestruck. As I watched the shower of creatures, vibrant with new life, I could feel the essence of the goddess. It was love, total love. She had loved so completely that she had given completely, holding nothing back for there was nothing she identified as "hers." I had been shown that it is pure love that gives itself over to every form it loves, and that every form is born of this love. She had demonstrated that the greatest gift a god or goddess gives is to take the form of whatever it loves and surrender to that reality. I knew then how we, as human beings, came to be and how it is that we carry goddess within, even when we do not know it.

I could feel that there was no loss for the goddess. She was still vibrantly alive in each of the creatures she had become, as alive as she had been before she took the dive into new form. And I sensed a pull somewhere deep within myself, telling me that I, too, carried the love that is the goddess. Yet I also felt disconnection, an inability to feel the love completely and to be in its surrender. I longed to reconnect, but in that moment I could not. With my emptiness I stood at the edge of the pond, surrounded by the life of the goddess, waiting for the time when I could accept her essence as my own and allow her to fully awaken within me.

◆

Martia Nelson offers personal readings for individuals wanting clarity and support as they open to true self. Readings can be done in person or by telephone. They are designed to:

- Strengthen your awareness of true self and life purpose
- Reveal untapped resources you carry within
- Apply the spiritual principles in this book to the issues in your life
- Help you take your next step in spiritual discovery

For a free brochure about personal readings, tapes, workshops, and talks, contact:

Martia Nelson
P.O. Box 1932
Sebastopol, CA 95473
(707) 823-4403

Nataraj Publishing

is committed to acting as a catalyst for change and transformation in the world by providing books and tapes on the leading edge in the fields of personal and social consciousness growth. "Nataraj" is a Sanskrit word referring to the creative, transformative power of the universe. For more information on our company, please contact us at:

Nataraj Publishing
1561 South Novato Blvd.
Novato, CA 94947
Phone: (415) 899-9666
Fax: (415) 899-9667

Other Books and Tapes
from Nataraj Publishing

Books

Living in the Light: A Guide to Personal and Planetary Transformation. By Shakti Gawain with Laurel King. The recognized classic on developing intuition and using it as a guide in living your life. (Trade paperback $9.95)

Living in the Light Workbook. By Shakti Gawain. Following up her bestseller, *Living in the Light.* Shakti has created a workbook to help us apply these principles to our lives in very practical ways. (Trade paperback $12.95)

Return to the Garden: A Journey of Discovery. By Shakti Gawain. Shakti reveals her path to self-discovery and personal power and shows us how to return to our personal garden and live on earth in a natural and balanced way. (Trade paperback $9.95)

Awakening: A Daily Guide to Conscious Living. By Shakti Gawain. A daily meditation guide that focuses on maintaining your spiritual center not just when you are in solitude, but when you are in the world, and especially, in relationships. (Trade paperback $8.95)

Embracing Our Selves: The Voice Dialogue Manual. By Drs. Hal and Sidra Stone. The highly acclaimed, groundbreaking work that explains the psychology of the selves and the Voice Dialogue method. (Trade paperback $12.95)

Embracing Each Other: Relationship as Teacher, Healer and Guide. By Drs. Hal and Sidra Stone. A compassionate guide to understanding and improving our relationships. The follow-up to the Stone's pioneering book on Voice Dialogue. (Trade paperback $11.95)

Maps to Ecstasy: Teachings of an Urban Shaman. By Gabrielle Roth with John Loudon. A modern shaman shows us how to reconnect to the vital energetic core of our being through dance, song, theater, writing, meditation, and ritual. (Trade paperback $9.95)

Notes from My Inner Child: I'm Always Here. By Tanha Luvaas. This deeply touching book puts us in contact with the tremendous energy and creativity of the inner child. (Trade paperback $8.95)

Coming Home: The Return to True Self. By Martia Nelson. A down-to-earth spiritual primer that explains how we can use the very flaws of our humanness to carry the vibrant energy of our true self and reach the potential that dwells in all of us. (Trade paperback $12.95)

Corporate Renaissance: Business as an Adventure in Human Development. By Rolf Osterberg. This groundbreaking book explodes the myth that a business's greatest asset is capital, and shows why employees must come first for businesses to succeed in the 90s. (Hardcover $18.95)

Passion to Heal: The Ultimate Guide to Your Healing Journey. By Echo Bodine. An invaluable guide to mapping out our individual journeys to health. (Trade paperback $14.95)

The Path of Transformation: How Healing Ourselves Can Change the World. By Shakti Gawain. Shakti gave us *Creative Visualization* in the 70s, *Living in the Light* in the 80s, and now *The Path of Transformation* for the 90s. Shakti's new bestseller delivers an inspiring and provocative message for the path of true transformation. (Trade paperback $9.95)

The Revelation: Our Crisis Is a Birth. By Barbara Marx Hubbard. An underground classic from one of the true prophets of our time. Hubbard offers an astonishing interpretation of the Book of Revelation, which reveals the consciousness required by the human race, not only to survive, but to blossom into full realization of its potentials. (Trade paperback 365 pgs. $16.95)

The Shadow in America: Reclaiming the Soul of a Nation. Edited by Jeremiah Abrams. Ten visionaries including bestselling authors Thomas Moore and Robert Bly discuss our nation's shadow and its role in gender relations, racism, politics, sexuality, addiction, and love. (Trade paperback $12.95)

Tapes

Living in the Light: Read by Shakti Gawain. Shakti reads her bestseller. (Two cassettes $15.95)

Developing Intuition. Shakti Gawain expands on the ideas about intuition she first discussed in *Living in the Light.* (One cassette $10.95)

The Path of Transformation: How Healing Ourselves Can Change the World. Shakti reads her inspiring new bestseller. (Two 70-minute cassettes $15.95)

To Place an Order

Call 1-800-949-1091.